Testimonials

Cheryl's writing is forthright, concise and relatable. Her ability to combine knowledge, practicality and empathy makes this book an invaluable resource and a testament to her impact and influence.

Her unwavering commitment to excellence is evident as she offers practical advice, real-life examples and actionable steps that resonate on a personal level and make for informative and thought-provoking reading. She creates a sense of camaraderie and offers authentic support and encouragement for parents who are navigating the complex and often dense landscape of education.

This book is not just an educational resource. It is a transformative and invaluable tool that empowers parents to take the lead, with confidence, and be responsible advocates for their children's education.

—Colleen Harkin, National Manager and Research Fellow, Institute of Public Affairs

A must-have resource for all parents with school-aged children. Cheryl has a unique and quirky writing style that invites you in with personal stories and tongue-in-cheek humour and then delivers the most honest and thought- provoking content.

The book helps the reader see school education in the only way that's right for now: through the eyes of a responsible and informed parent.

Cheryl has woven her own journey as a parent into a rich tapestry of invaluable information, useful snippets and brilliant coffee break conversation topics. *Your Children* tackles some sensitive topics about different school systems, teacher roles and responsibilities, and legal mumbo jumbo is broken down into easy to remember lessons. The fact that Cheryl is both a parent and a teacher allows a very rare insight into the world of education.

—Michael Ray, Solo Dad and Author, Melbourne, Australia

Cheryl Lacey has written a very interesting and intriguing book that invites us to think differently about education. Written for parents, her insights, ideas, and activities are presented with her own personal experiences to make this a very readable book.

—Professor Andrew P. Johnson, Literacy Scholar, Minnesota State University, USA

Cheryl Lacey's *Your Children: Take the Lead on Their Education* is a must read for all parents and expectant mothers and fathers. She provides valuable, practical, first-hand counsel on the importance of education and the critical role parents play in navigating their child's education. The book is a terrific resource.

—Dr. Michael Gargano, Jr, Ed.D. University Executive Leadership, Connecticut, USA

Cheryl's courageous yearning for a successful school education is right on the money. Her advocacy for parents and their children will enrich families and the communities in which they reside. Cheryl is the teacher's teacher. To see why, you must read this book for yourself.

—Howard Hutchins, Parent, Granddad, Great Granddad, Principal for a Day, Businessman

Your Children

TAKE THE LEAD ON THEIR EDUCATION

CHERYL LACEY

Published in 2023 by Connor Court Publishing Pty Ltd

Copyright © 2023 by Cheryl Lacey

All rights reserved. No part of this book may be reproduced, stored in a retrieval system, or transmitted in any form or by any means, electronic, mechanical, photocopying, recording, or otherwise, without written permission from the publisher.

ISBN: 978-1-922815-59-0

First Edition

Connor Court Publishing Pty Ltd
PO Box 7257
Redland Bay QLD 4165
sales@connorcourt.com

www.connorcourtpublishing.com.au

Design and Typesetting: Lorie DeWorken

Cover Photo: Mish Winters

Printed in Australia

Dedication

To Somraudee and Sze Ting,

Thank you for the honour and privilege of being your 'Mother Hen' and for letting me scatter your lives through these pages.

You are my heroes. I will always love you both 'too much'.

In Memory of Dad and John

God bless.

Acknowledgements

Home will always be Australia and the US, where strength and vulnerability can safely reside and where loved ones patiently walk beside us as we regain lost or stolen dignity. My thanks to family, friends and colleagues who help make this a reality.

Particular thanks to Alexandra Chapman, Sharon Rondeau, Valda Bonnie and Tom Minchin for providing a safe place *to think out loud*.

To John and Marg Uren; thank you for choosing teaching as a vocation and influencing my life path.

To the strangers and acquaintances whose paths I have crossed in more than 50 countries; thank you for the fleeting moments of learning and teaching.

To my publisher, Anthony Cappello and editor, Janette Parr; there wouldn't be a book without your support and talent.

To Simon Brown, Maria Tsakalakis-Coate, James McHale, Wendy Marquenie, Michael Ray, Professor Andrew P. Johnson, Dr. Michael Gargano Jr, Colleen Harkin, Michael Partis and Dr. Deborah M. Vereen – critical friends and purveyors of rich and stimulating dialogue. Thank you.

To my forever mentors; our friendship is gold as we *realise ideas*. Thank you.

To my new friends at the Institute of Family Therapy Malta; we are pioneers in teaching and learning about parental alienation. Change is on the horizon. Bless you.

To my New York sister, Angela Fressle and dearly missed friend, Maree Rizk (deceased); thank you for choosing motherhood as your life's work and for holding my hand in motherhood.

To Clifton; unconditional love, always and forever.

And one final word of gratitude to all those I have named and those I haven't. The spaces between my words and the thoughts between my sentences are yours. Without your perspective, there would be no difference to make.

Such is the nature of education and life. We can do neither alone.

Stay safe, and God bless.

Preface

In Australia, at the time of Federation, there were compulsory education acts in all colonies and many schools were established as a result. Parents, and the communities to which they belonged, worked together and were responsible for education.

No child was left behind. A fair and equal opportunity was afforded children from families with lesser means and those from more fortunate family settings.

Beyond primary schooling, there was no barrier to further education – whether it was acquired in academic institutions or by other means.

To be educated: that was the vision of our forefathers and mothers. They built our schools and universities, our places of worship and our homes. They built our nation.

Over time, though, a new narrative emerged. There were suggestions that government and bureaucrats could do a better job. Gradually, parents and the communities to which they belonged were seduced into forfeiting their responsibilities for educating the young.

By reading this book, you've joined a brave community of change makers - mothers and fathers, grandparents and carers, educational leaders and teachers – who want to see that trend reversed.

Raising children is an honour and a privilege. Parents' responsibilities must be sincerely encouraged and never weakened.

About This Book

This book is for you if you're a parent, a grandparent or anyone who has family attending school.

This book, or should I say, *your* book, is all about one major lesson. Scribble and sketch, circle and highlight as you read. And if you have a question, call me. Seriously!

When you reach the end, taking the lead in your children's education will be a breeze.

Sharpen your pencil and let's get started.

Contents

Preface vii

School Life Today 1

School Taught Me.... 3
    Who Will Raise My Children?   5
    Your Vantage Point   8
    You're It!   10
    Pinky Promise   10

Great Expectations 13
    The Little Grey Case   15
    You're Responsible: No 'Buts'   16
    Do Your Homework   19
    Parents Leading Learning   21

Our 'Learning to Lead' Agenda 23
    Lessons From The Sandpit   24
    Lessons From The Classroom   25
    Lessons From The Boardroom   26
    Wrap Up   27

Part 1: Lessons From The Sandpit 29
    Lesson 1: A Shared Language of Agreement   33
    Lesson 2: School Education: What's the Purpose?   47
    Lesson 3: Families, Fairness and Difference   58
    Lesson 4: Play by the Rules   69
    Lesson 5: Home Life at School   81
    Learnings from Part 1   94

Part 2: Lessons From The Classroom 95
    Lesson 1: Schools and the Philosophy of Education   99
    Lesson 2: Pedagogy and Personalised Learning   112
    Lesson 3: Those Who Teach   123
    Lesson 4: Curriculum Matters   136
    Lesson 5: Reading and Beyond   151
    Lesson 6: Getting Down to Basics   168

Lesson 7: Measure That!	181
Lesson 8: School Comes at a Cost	195
Lesson 9: Big Tech, Little Tech	205
Lesson 10: School Days	214
Learnings from Part 2	226

Part 3: Lessons From The Boardroom **227**

Lesson 1: Country Wide Local Schools	231
Lesson 2: Ownership and Collaboration	240
Lesson 3: Strategy and Change	248
Lesson 4: Education Services	259
Learnings from Part 3	270

Taking the Lead **271**

A Final Word **281**

Your Legacy	283
Keep in Touch	285
First Principles on Education™	287
Glossary	289

School Life Today

13. Graduation. Your children progress through school regardless of their ability and graduate at the end.

12. Government Funding. This goes directly to the school and might not be applied to your children's needs or wants.

11. Teacher Choice. You rarely get to choose who teaches your children.

9. Decision Making. Principals and the school board make decisions at the local school level.

10. Teaching Staff. Most are university graduates with general degrees in education.

8. Family Life. You must fit your life around the school calendar.

7. Standard Of Instruction. You accept what the school offers, regardless of teacher expertise.

6. Curriculum. There is no agreed specified curriculum.

5. School Calendar. Schools are open for standard instruction for 7hrs – 5 days per week for 40 weeks of the year.

4. Compulsory Attendance. You must ensure your children attend school when it is open for standard instruction.

3. School Choice. Your children can attend a State government school for free. You can school your children at home at your expense or you can pay for your children to attend a non-government school.

2. School Life Begins Here. Your children must be enrolled in a State registered school from the age of 5 to 17 years (approx.).

1. Responsibility. Chances are you're like most parents: you're unclear about your responsibility for your children's education.

School Taught Me...

You've achieved everything you wanted in life and more. Right?
Full credit goes to the school you attended – your teachers and the education your school provided.

For you, school was perfect in every way. It prepared you for a healthy life, work and hobbies, and taught you how to manage relationships and finances, success and disappointment and so much more. Right?

The truth is different: school *didn't* prepare you for everything; going to school didn't teach you everything. It wasn't meant to.

The same is true for your children.

School offers a mixture of fabulous, great, good, ok, not-so-good, dull and downright dreary moments – just like life itself. But let's put these aside for a moment. Schools have one genuine purpose. They're intended to weave one very important thread into life's education tapestry.

Schools provide a place for your children to be taught an agreed curriculum by capable teachers.

Your role is to make sure you know the extent of the educational value your children's school provides and how well your children are learning. You must also know what to do when the school and the learning don't meet your expectations. Only then can you be confident that the education provided at school is what your children need, rather than what others say your children ought to have.

Let's be honest with each other right now. They're your children. So you're it! *Numero uno*! The team leader for *their* education. No excuses. No questions asked.

Are you ready?

Who Will Raise My Children?

Who will raise my children? This was my first and only thought at the moment I was diagnosed with breast cancer. At 45, with two daughters, aged 12 and 4, I was more terrified for them than I was for myself.

Somraudee, my eldest, was born in Thailand and was 3 years and 10 months old when I became her mum. Sze Ting, born in Hong Kong, was almost 1 year old when I became her mum, four years later.

How could it be possible, I thought, for it all to be lost so soon?

The diagnosis marked another turning point for me. I finally understood what was driving my view of education, the role of schools and those who worked in them.

At that point, my future was uncertain. One thing, though, was clear: people working in schools, whether directly or indirectly, wouldn't shout out, 'My duty of care extends to raising your children if anything should happen to you'. And neither should they.

Schools aren't homes. Those who work in schools aren't parents to your children. Raising children isn't done through a 'partnership' between your home and your children's school or between you and your children's teachers. Instead, you have a 'relationship' with the school and the teachers.

You might be wondering about the difference between the two.

Essentially, I do not believe that everyone involved with your children has equal responsibility for them – and that's as it should be. In my view, it's not a question of 'partnership'. There is, however, an ever-evolving ebb and flow of people, knowledge and beliefs that have many and varied relationships with, and influence on, you and your children.

And it's the nature of this relationship we need to qualify.

Parents are responsible for raising children and raising them in their own way. My view has remained constant: I've raised my girls on my terms and on behalf of their biological parents.

Schools provide education services. But there is a tremendous difference between respectful appreciation of those services and unconditional trust in them.

Respectful appreciation of the role of a teacher and the role of a parent has always been an intrinsic compass for me. This is probably because, as a child, I always knew what I wanted to be – a mum and a teacher.

When I began teaching in 1989, however, I wasn't fully prepared for the experiences I was about to have and where they would take me. The same was the case a decade later when I became a mum.

At the time of the cancer diagnosis, I had already invested twenty years in trying to tie a ribbon of mutual respect around the home-school relationship, through teaching, radio broadcasting, publishing, advisory work, business ownership and parenting.

It became clear that everything I had done and experienced during those twenty years was merely an apprenticeship. The real work was just about to begin.

Drawing on my experience, I took a dive into the depths of humanity to try to understand how the power imbalance between home and school had evolved, how the values of faith and family had been undermined and how we had fallen, unconsciously, into an *unhealthy co-dependency with government* with regard to school education and the raising of our children.

School education is highly emotional.

You're about to explore the fundamental principles I believe will serve you well as the leading advocate for your children's education. I've also woven into the text personal anecdotes about some of my experiences as a parent, an international educator and writer of more than 30 years, and a few stories about a little girl still growing up.

To present them as a 'tell-all' would be inappropriate, and not to include both successes and examples of poor judgement would be insincere. I hope I have landed at a place somewhere in the middle.

That's the place I call trust.

I trust you'll learn enough about me to trust in my intention and my hope for you. And that is for you to be equipped to do for your children all you can, when you can, with what you have and know.

Thankfully, more than a decade after my diagnosis, I'm still here, raising my beautiful girls, teaching, and remaining dedicated to sharing what I have learned with you.

Your Vantage Point

To be honest, I don't know what questions you might have about education. And I don't know how much experience you have with regard to school education.

What I *do* know is that you're likely to view schools through your own memories and from the vantage point of your childhood. Do you recall your favourite teachers and the respect you had for them? They held positions of authority. They knew you, taught you well, expected the best from you and introduced you to new ideas and new ways of thinking. And you probably remember those not-so-good teachers, too.

Most of us tend to relate to school in this way. Your experiences as a student won't inform your expectations today; neither will they help you understand how teachers go about fulfilling their responsibilities. You need a new vantage point. It's time to view school education through fresh eyes. You're not a child anymore.

Your children will be in school between the ages of about 5 and 18. That covers most of their childhood years. School will have an enormous influence on their lives and quite an impact on your life, too.

Thirteen years of school might seem a long time but it goes by very quickly. You'll cry on their first day, if you haven't already, and you'll cry at their graduation. Before you know it, everything they have learned in school will be the luggage they take on their life journey. There'll also be some extra baggage.

The last thing I want for you is regret. School life goes by faster than you imagine, especially if you juggle work and more than one child. So please don't hesitate. Jump right in and welcome your new vantage point.

As someone who works in education, I can assure you that teachers and school leaders see school education from a very different vantage point, even if they are also parents. Their view of what's taking place depends on their position and their responsibility in a given situation at a given moment. They won't automatically look at situations that affect your children from your vantage point.

That's why it's so important to relinquish a view of school that's based on your childhood experiences. It won't always be easy but it's essential to remind yourself constantly to do so. You'll be surprised at what's revealed when your stored memories are stirred.

You might remember a time you were reprimanded in front of your peers, or the moment your achievements were celebrated by a teacher you respected. Every school-related experience will influence your thinking and how you might initially react to your children's experiences.

If you catch yourself acting in blind faith, or making harsh criticisms, pause and remind yourself that you're taking the lead. You need to see what schools offer your children and what they don't.

You need to see school education in the only way that's right for now: through the eyes of a responsible and informed parent.

There's no going back.

You're It!

Honestly, you're like every other parent with children already at school or about to start. You're a citizen of the world of school education.

There'll be barbecues and family gatherings full of chatter about schools and comparisons between schools. Some parents will boast about how great their children's school is; others will say very little. Some will be involved – boots and all – sitting on every committee, and on a 'first name, best friend' basis with all the teachers; some will rarely enter the school gates. Other parents will develop a healthy balance somewhere in between. And you'll be among them.

The reason you choose to participate in school education the way you do will make all the difference in how you tackle the number one lesson in this book. Honesty.

Be honest with yourself. Expect honesty from your children. And demand honesty from schools and those who influence what goes on behind the school gates.

That's what it's all about. Honesty!

It doesn't matter which school your child attends. If honesty is missing, there's nothing to be gained by choosing a school for reasons of family tradition, reputation, convenience or connections.

You're the one who will make the difference. It's up to you to keep yourself and everyone else honest.

Got it? Good.

Pinky Promise

The most serious and sacred promise in the history of the world is the pinky promise. You know the one – where you link your pinky finger to the pinky finger of someone you trust.

My pinky promise to you is this: *I'll provide you with the advice and the tools you need so you'll be equipped to expect and receive nothing but the best possible education for your children.*

I aim to make sure you're confident about holding the number one position in your children's education. And, in time, your children will thank you for it.

Everything you are about to read comes directly from personal experience.

You see, even though I'm an educator and have worked with thousands of school leaders and teachers, I had to learn how to hold the number one position for my children too.

And so can you.

Being frank is your most powerful tool. Always be open, honest and direct.

And don't sugar coat. Sugar coating results in acceptance of the unacceptable. Please don't confuse this with compromise; that's something entirely different. Sugar coating is pretending that something is OK when, clearly, it's not.

If we're going to be completely honest with each other – and we are – it's fair to say that many students have succeeded and many dedicated teachers have served well in school settings. It's also important to point out that many have not.

The consequence of sugar coating is that your voice, my voice and the voice of every parent aren't heard.

And they must be heard!

You mustn't sugar coat anything. Promise?

At times, staying the course will feel uncomfortable. But allowing people to assert unacceptable authority over your children feels worse.

Be honest. Be open. Be direct. Be frank.

Your children need you. We all need you.

They're your children. You can and you will demand the best for your children. Pinky promise.

Great Expectations

Homes are places of learning and teaching. You're contributing to your children's education more than you possibly realise.

There'll be days when you notice big or small changes in their abilities and behaviours. Some days you'll be distracted and won't see much; on others, you'll have *great expectations* of their performance. It's all part of parenting. It's also a huge part of teaching and learning.

We've become so accustomed to handing our children over to others, especially in schools, that we can short-change ourselves. You might not earn a living as a teacher but let's get one thing straight: you help your children to learn. You are your children's first and forever teacher. That can never be taken from you.

Remember to appreciate what you do for your children. Even when you get things wrong or have a bad day, your children learn from you.

The same applies to extended family and friends. You have a significant role in shaping how your children react to the positive and not-so-good influences on their learning.

Isn't that terrific?

The Little Grey Case

In my first year of school, Dad gave me a little grey case with the initials CL engraved on it. It has been with me ever since. Inside, there's an array of keepsakes from my school years: a picture I drew for a competition but which mum never mailed; a collection of pen pal letters from Debbie, my best friend in primary school; reports and photos; and a score card from ten pin bowling – on my first date. I've even kept my swap cards. They're all part of my treasure trove of memories.

Other treasures were added more recently. Dad passed away in early 2020. Among his belongings were schoolbooks and report cards from his school years, dating back to the 1940s. Not only are they significant in appreciating Dad's life but they also add to the historical context of how schooling has evolved and how the relationship between parents and educators has changed.

Don't underestimate the value of what you think might be the small things you do. They often become the big stuff. If you haven't done it already, I urge you to start a treasure box of keepsakes from your children's school education. My daughters each have one. It's never too late to begin.

You'll never know the impact a treasure box of keepsakes might have on how your children interact with schools when they become school parents.

You're Responsible: No 'Buts'

If you suspect this book is not for you, you're wrong. My purpose in writing it was to make one thing absolutely clear: *Your children's education is in your hands.*

Everything that does or doesn't happen in school, with regard to your children, is your business. *Everything!*

If you're feeling a little hesitant, consider this. Teachers, principals, politicians and bureaucrats who have influence over your children's school education are *not* responsible for your children when school ends each day, week, term or year – and certainly not when school education ends forever.

Who is responsible? You are.

When I say this to parents, there's usually a 'Yes, but...' response.

'Yes, but my children have great teachers. They're nice. I trust them.'

This isn't about teachers' personalities or teachers being nice. It's about doing what is right by your children. Trusting teachers is how parents *should* feel – but trust must be earned and demonstrated. Teachers are paid to serve you and your children. They are paid to teach essential knowledge and skills, which your children can build on, throughout their lives, according to their own life choices. Your role is to make sure this happens and that anything that distracts from laying those essential foundations is removed.

'Yes, but my children go to a private school. I have made this investment to get the best possible education for my children.'

Your authority does not change, regardless of the school your children attend. Currently, the state in which you live registers every school and every teacher. Paying school fees doesn't change that. Money doesn't buy honesty and money alone doesn't guarantee the desired outcome. Parents who pay additional fees should be more vigilant in monitoring the services provided. They're absolutely right. They've invested in getting the best possible education.

'Yes, but I don't know enough about school education today, and I didn't complete Year 12.'

That's precisely why you have this book. I'm here to help. You're about to learn everything you'll need to take the lead in your children's education. You'll read about how schools work and where you fit in. You'll learn to establish boundaries between raising your children and having others do so under the false pretence that they have greater authority over your children than you do.

'Yes, but I'm also a teacher.'

That's even more reason why you should be reading this book. It will help you view school education from your vantage point as a parent. It will also inform your perspective as an educator, so that any decisions you make will be in the best interests of other parents and their children.

'Yes, but what if I'm the only parent who thinks the way I do?'

How others regard what you think, what you know or don't know and what questions you have doesn't matter. Remember, this is all about being honest with yourself and being the centre of influence for your children.

Don't hesitate to ask, learn and, if necessary, teach. You might not always get things right but that doesn't take away your position. You have the authority. Don't ever apologise for being a parent and demanding what's necessary.

'Yes, but I'm too busy.'

We are all busy in one way or another. Taking the lead doesn't necessarily mean doing all the work. This is where networks, grandparents and other support come into play.

You might be busy but you aren't too busy to have authority. You'll be able to determine the support you and your children need. You're the parent; remember that.

'*Yes, but my other children have turned out just fine. I just want them to be happy.*'

That's fantastic. I say the same about my two girls. That's precisely the point. We all want happiness for our children and that includes preventing unnecessary unhappiness.

Consider this. When you're faced with unhappy children, the worst possible option is to do nothing. Taking the lead and asserting your rightful authority might be a totally new experience for you. All I can say is, go for it.

Let's be clear. You won't always get it right.

But don't make excuses about why you can't try.

Do Your Homework

Now is probably the best time to warn you: *there will be homework.* Don't worry; it's almost certainly not what you think.

We've just been talking about responsibility. But what does that mean?

I can honestly say that, despite everything I learned from my parents and in my role as an educator, it wasn't until I became a mum that I really started to understand it. You probably felt the same.

As a parent, you love your children unconditionally and you know you're entirely responsible for them. At the same time, you possibly have no idea what's needed to fulfil that responsibility until it's needed.

That's what I mean by homework. You can only ever work with who you are and what you've learned at the precise moment you are called upon to take the lead. And that version of you is constantly changing.

To become a parent, I spent five years on IVF, without success. Then it took a decade to go through the process of intercountry adoption.

And when I saw the absolute control government employees had over children I might want to adopt, it opened my eyes to the power governments have over so many other areas of family life.

When I finally became a mother, my 'message to self' was:

Before they begin school, you must have ample time at home with your daughters, to bond with them. If you don't, they'll never be yours; they'll be swept up in a school bureaucracy that will undermine your responsibilities and their future.

Perhaps you've thought the same thing.

Raising children and managing the political influences that affect your beliefs, your plans and your daily life is what I mean by 'home' work.

You and your surroundings might change and the influences might change; being a parent, though, is a constant. As your children grow older, you'll learn different ways to protect, advise, nurture and, where necessary, reprimand them.

They're your children – for life.

As I mentioned earlier, you'll need to have a pencil ready. I hope that, as you work through this book – your book – it will be full of your notes, scribbles, questions, underlinings and anything else that will help you thrive.

Respond honestly. Learn all you can. Don't be afraid to disagree or ask questions. I don't have all the answers and haven't included all I could about school education. There must be room for you to navigate what you know and what you need to learn next.

Deep down, it isn't really homework at all. It's the path you choose to take the lead in your children's school education.

Parents Leading Learning

As you begin to appreciate your value as the number one influencer of your children's education, you'll take more notice of how other parents are tackling similar challenges and opportunities. Your relationship with them will evolve in many ways.

You'll see the parent community's confidence, ability and willingness to participate become increasingly evident.

Scattered throughout the book are topic ideas for what I call *'APLL'* groups. APLL stands for *Australian Parents Leading Learning*.

You might prefer to a *Parents Leading Learning 'PLL group'* and personalise it with your location; perhaps a Brisbane group *'BPLL'* or a more local context, a Gold Coast group *'GCPLL'*. You might set up a group beyond Australia. A *United States* 'USPLL Group', or *London Parents Leading Learning* 'LPLL'.

Anyway, the idea behind them is to encourage the growth of an independent supportive network, made up of you and other school parents.

You don't need to be a 'first time-first year' school parent to benefit from this book or to gain something valuable from an APLL group. Every school parent benefits when ideas, concerns and questions about their children's school education are shared.

Our 'Learning to Lead' Agenda

This section is in three parts. Each part includes a series of lessons to help you be the most well-informed parent at your children's school.

Wow! Imagine if every parent at your school were to read this book. That would add up to a powerful movement for change.

PART 1: LESSONS FROM THE SANDPIT

This will cover *The Big 5* – five lessons containing the essential elements that lay the foundations for being a well-informed school parent.

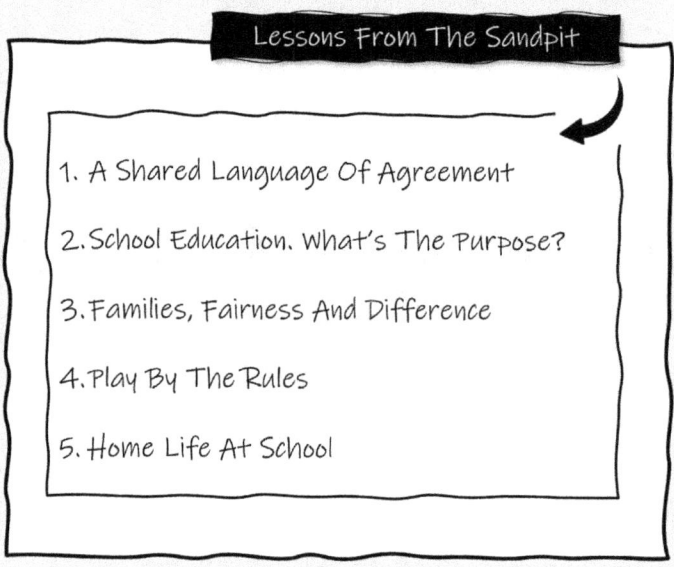

Lessons From The Sandpit

1. A Shared Language Of Agreement
2. School Education, What's The Purpose?
3. Families, Fairness And Difference
4. Play By The Rules
5. Home Life At School

PART 2: LESSONS FROM THE CLASSROOM

In this part, we're concerned with the nuts and bolts of schools. Each of the ten lessons is a snapshot of day-to-day issues that affect your children's school education and family life.

Don't worry about what you already know or don't know. I've considered busy parents, single parents, grandparents and the blending of home-work-school and family life. I'm sure there's enough breadth for you to pick up the key intentions of each lesson, regardless of your current situation.

Here's a preview of what we'll explore...

PART 3: LESSONS FROM THE BOARDROOM

By the time you reach this final part, you'll be ready to become the centre of influence – for your children, for the parents of other children and, perhaps, for those in your extended family or workplace.

The purpose of these four lessons is to apply what's been covered in the sandpit and classroom lessons so as to bring about local change. It might not happen immediately, or in all areas, but there will be change.

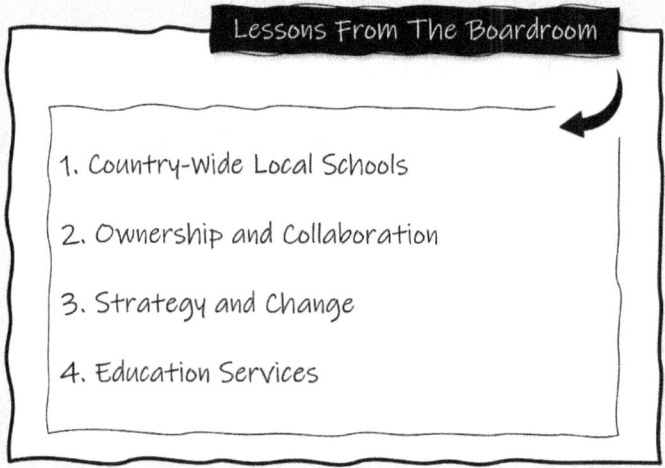

Reading this book is one thing; achieving something for your children's education is another. I'm confident you will be a powerful player in the essential movement for change that inspired me to write this book.

If you're up for it, you can become the driving force that makes the difference between an institution that offers a mediocre school education and the ultimate *School of Distinction*™.

And the best thing about schools getting a makeover is that every family – including yours – will benefit.

It's great to have your support.

WRAP UP

To 'wrap up' each lesson, I will provide a summary of the key message. You'll find a list of these at the end of Part 1, Part 2 and Part 3, as a brief outline of what you've learned.

Suppose your interest or curiosity leads you to tap in and out across lessons, instead of reading them in sequence. In that case, you'll see key learnings still to explore. Essentially, they're a quick check-in on what's been covered and an easy reference for conversations and review.

Here's a wrap up of what you've read so far.

Wrap Up

- As a parent, you have the right to fulfil your responsibility to raise your children

- Schools provide a place for your children to be taught an agreed curriculum by capable teachers.

Part 1:
Lessons From The Sandpit

Lessons From The Sandpit

1. A Shared Language Of Agreement

2. School Education. What's The Purpose?

3. Families, Fairness And Difference

4. Play By The Rules

5. Home Life At School

The sandpit is one of the most popular environments for children to learn to play alongside others.

And, if you're like me and almost every other parent I know, you've had what I call *the sandpit moment*. It goes a little like this.

Your child is playing alongside another. Someone throws sand and both children begin to cry. Your immediate reaction is to protect your child. The other child's parent reacts in the same way. Usually, there is a congenial outcome and both children learn valuable lessons about personal space, resilience or getting along with others.

But it doesn't always work that way. What happens when the sandpit is in the school grounds, and you aren't there? How do you react when you hear what happened? Things change, in a big way, once your children are at school. It isn't long before the sandpit is replaced with all kinds of scenarios where you are absent and someone else steps in.

Regardless of the scenario, some things never change. You'll always be the parent and your right to support your children should always outweigh the right of any 'other' who steps in. How to handle that situation is the challenge.

Let's begin with the essentials.

LESSON 1:
A Shared Language of Agreement

How many times have you been in a conversation only to become confused when a word or phrase is used differently from the way you'd expect?

Here's one! *Cool*. I bet there have been times you've used it to describe something trendy, rather than the weather.

How about *sick*? Most parents would take this to mean 'ill'. Your children probably use it instead of fabulous. Both meanings are correct. It's all about context. And you have to get context right to communicate effectively.

Almost everything we do involves language. Every day we're immersed in words and the concepts and ideas they represent. Without them, human interaction would have little meaning.

Your children constantly take concepts and ideas into their classrooms and bring others home. Some you'll discuss and some you won't. Some will impress you; others might shock you. Just remember to be clear about what is meant by certain words or concepts when you have conversations with your children.

The same applies to any communication between you, other parents and school staff, whether it involves meetings or informal chats, newsletters, notices and consent forms, school policies and board reports, or website content.

IT'S NOT THAT COMMON

What might appear logical can often confuse, especially when meanings change. Communication breaks down and there's unexpected conflict. What you set out to achieve becomes increasingly difficult, and the last thing you want is to have your children caught in the middle. After all, you're only trying to help.

You can probably relate to the following situation:

For years students took 'readers' home from school to improve their reading and local libraries were a source of great interest, especially for research and borrowing non-fiction books. Now, 'readers' refer to the person reading, 'non-fiction' books are 'factual texts' and students borrow 'take home' books from school libraries and classrooms.

It's taken decades for teachers to use the word 'readers' in the same way. As for 'non-fiction' and 'factual texts', the jury's out. Who would have thought teachers in the same school, region or country could use words like 'reader', 'fiction' and 'factual' differently?

If teachers aren't crystal clear in their communication, no wonder parents become frustrated, relationships become strained and educational goals are more difficult to achieve. We've all encountered situations like these.

Let's delve a little deeper.

The phrase *common language* might be one you're familiar with. Teachers often use it to describe something that's needed to improve school performance. Without a common language, teachers believe there are too many differences between teaching and learning goals across the school and a mismatch between stated objectives and what needs to be taught to achieve them.

I agree with their sentiment about inconsistency. However, I strongly believe it doesn't go far enough. A common language is just the first of *three* layers required for effective communication.

Layer 1: Common Language

For us it's English.

Layer 2: Common Understanding

We can't just use words randomly. We need to understand the words, phrases and concepts we're using.

Layer 3: Shared Language of Agreement

We need to be able to use words correctly. Because words, phrases and concepts can have more than one meaning, we must be sure we're using them in a way that is clear to everyone involved in the communication.

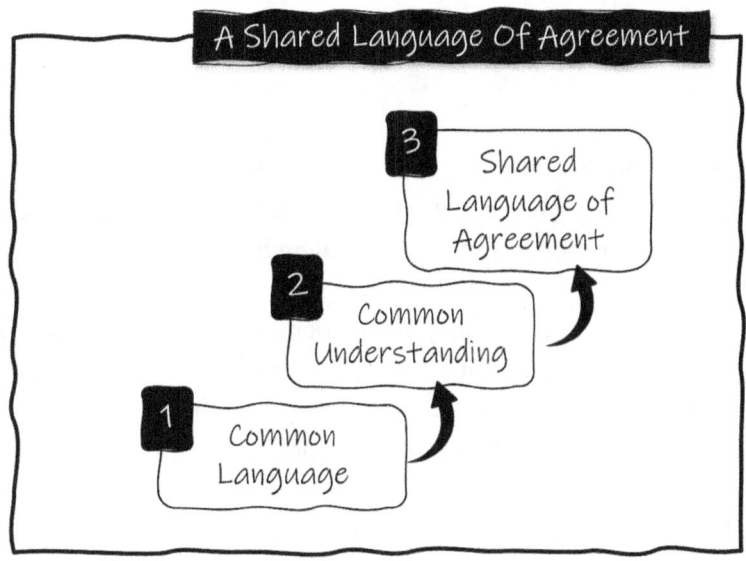

A shared language of agreement is just that. When the meaning of a word, phrase or concept is agreed, for the purpose of the conversation you are having, misunderstandings are diminished. Effective communication requires you to reach this third layer, in all interactions on all matters.

That's the way to achieve clarity, talk things through and get things done.

THE WHOLE CHILD: NOW THAT'S A CONCEPT WORTH EXPLORING

Your children are so capable. Every day, they learn something new about themselves, about managing daily life and about preparing for a future that's yet to unfold.

How strange! As I was typing, this phrase popped into my head: 'You're not the boss of me.'

Do you recall hearing that from your children or saying it yourself as a youngster?

Now, as a parent, you know that being responsible for your children doesn't mean having total control over them. Perhaps that's why the statement came to mind.

The concept of 'the whole child', often referred to in school education settings, suggests otherwise. Are you familiar with it?

The 'whole child approach to education' is intended to give children the foundation they need to become well-rounded, healthy individuals. Schools that take this approach believe they can equip *your children* with the education and essential life skills required for them to reach their full potential.

As an educator, I see that it has far-reaching implications for school education. As a parent, more importantly, it terrifies me. The reason for my fears can be stated simply: there is no shared language of agreement. In other words, the meaning, interpretation and application of the concept are not the same for everyone. A quick Internet search will confirm that.

For now, let's look at these two common interpretations.

THE WHOLE CHILD - CONCEPT ONE

Some, but not all, research into this concept of the whole child appears to suggest that many children live unfortunate lives – as a result of poverty or poor parenting on one hand or due to being spoiled or leading a life not worth living on the other. The assumption is that the role of school education is to remedy these problems. It seems government, researchers and bureaucracy know best – and 'best' knowledge involves giving schools greater authority and recognition in all areas of child development – that is, in the *whole* of the child's life.

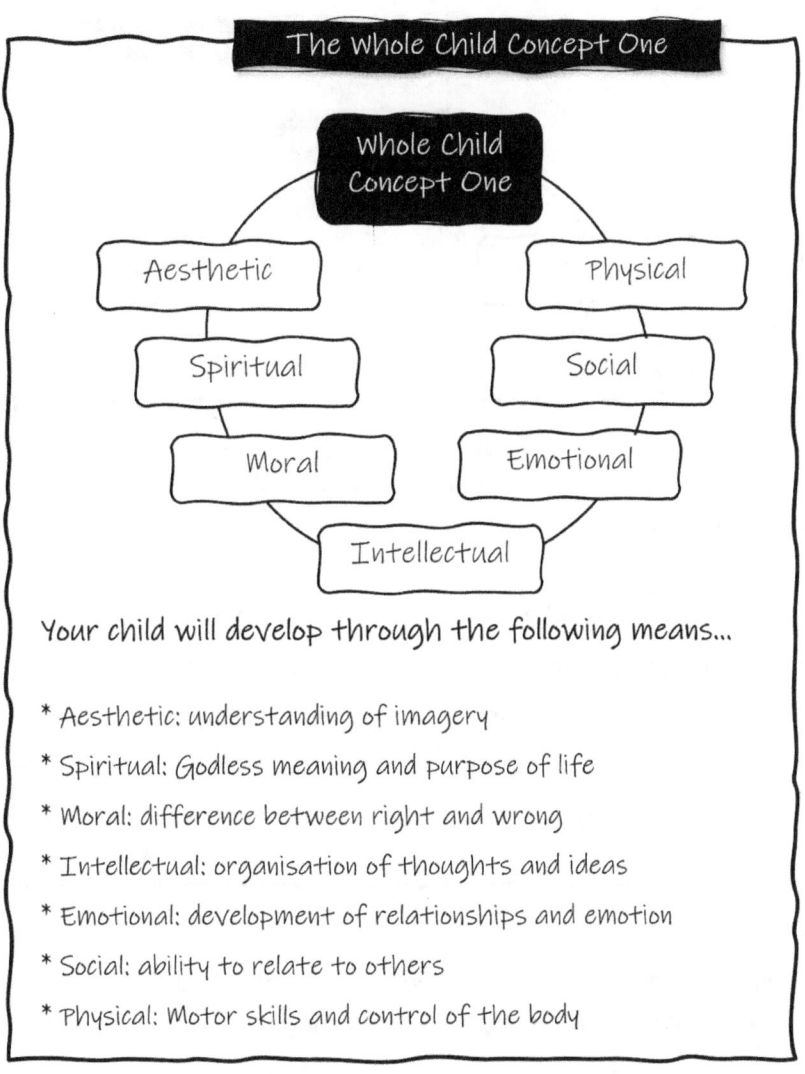

THE WHOLE CHILD - CONCEPT TWO

In this concept of the whole child, the focus seems to be on the environment in which your children learn, whether indoors, outdoors or online. These surroundings include all the social and cultural influences that operate wherever your children learn and are taught. We could celebrate these key elements; they sing to parents wanting the best for their children. Likewise, we could also be concerned, as they are open to interpretation. If they were stretched to include areas beyond what you believe schools' involvement should be or if they were narrowly addressed, the implications could be far-reaching.

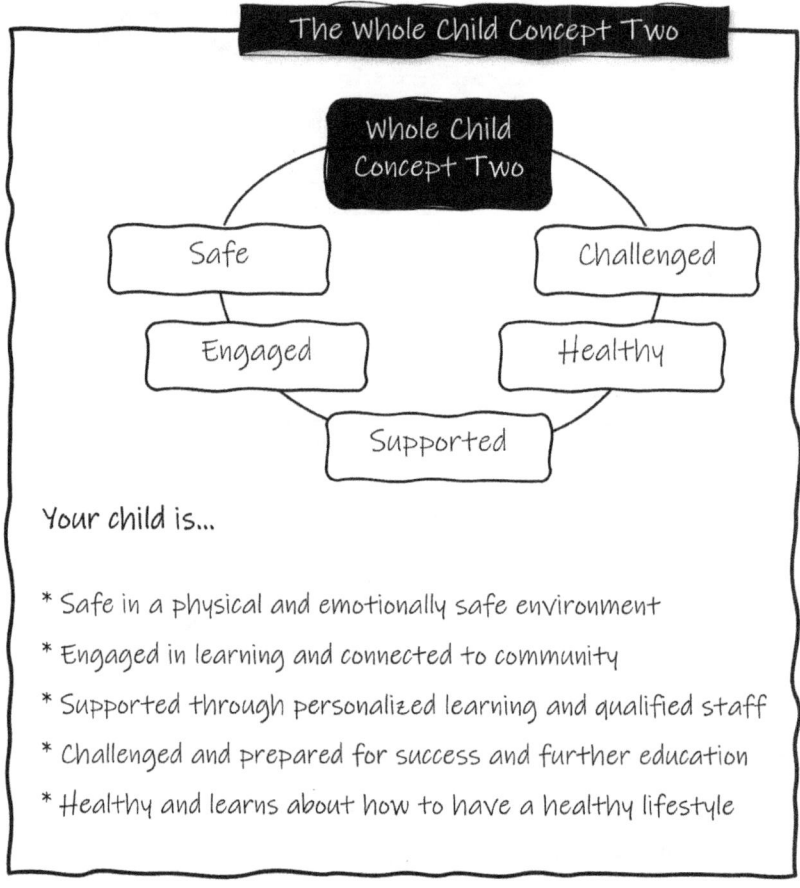

There is quite a difference between these two concepts, don't you agree? And just as homes are not the same, neither are schools, as workplaces or places of learning.

The truth is, all *those where, when, what, how* and *by whom* moments in your children's education can never be fully known or controlled – by you or anyone else.

Being responsible for your children's education doesn't mean having the perfect setting to do it all on your own. Surely, the same applies to schools.

'You're not the boss of me', is pretty powerful don't you think?

Keep this front of mind as you read the book and continue to take notes on your thoughts about *where, when, what, how* and *by whom* your children are educated.

SCHOOL: A WORD WORTH EXPLORING

Have you ever wondered about the genuine meaning of 'school'? What possibly seems really obvious at first might be worth exploring, especially if taking the lead, as a school parent, is the goal. Agreed?

From now on, I would like your understanding of 'school' to be *a place of learning.* That sounds about right. Notice, though, there's no mention of teaching. Let's go a bit further. What about 'schooling'? How does that compare?

Schooling is *instruction received at school.* Aha! Now we're getting somewhere. Let's keep going. Instruction is *the act of teaching*. Combining the three, we can say that a school is a *place where teaching and learning occur*. In other words, teaching and learning must go together. Let's add one more definition for good measure. Education is *the act of teaching and learning.*

You might be thinking, 'What's the big deal?' or 'This is all too hard!'

Believe it or not, although schools influence family life, confusion over what happens in schools and who's responsible for what is the main cause of almost all the anxiety I've experienced as a school parent. That's not what I want for you.

You've just read how a shared language of agreement positions everyone for a better chance of success. It's such an important principle. You also read about the difference between partnerships and relationships.

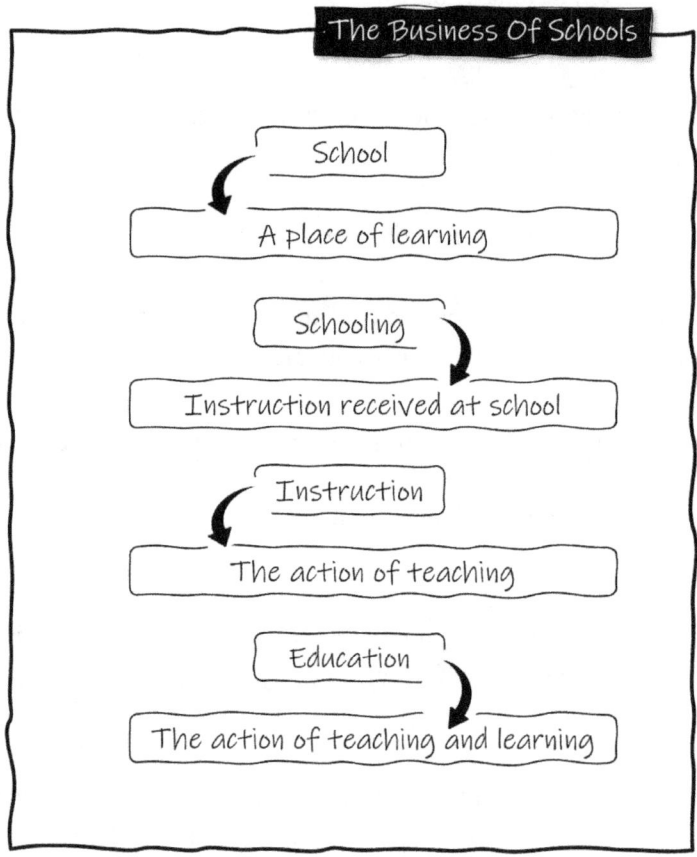

As you continue to explore learning, teaching and the purpose of schools, the difference between your responsibilities and those of school employees will become more evident. Your confidence will grow, too.

Ultimately, the language we use influences our communication and our relationships. We achieve our desired outcomes more effectively when we all understand and agree on our responsibilities and direction.

And that means beginning with a shared language of agreement.

MARGINS AND MARK UPS

At the end of the book, you'll find a glossary. You won't find the word 'sick', but the terms 'school' and 'education' are there. I've also included words that will help with communication between you and your children's teachers. Some will seem obvious; others might surprise.

As you're reading, use underlining, highlighting or margin notes to mark up any useful words or statements.

Your aim is clear communication. That means you'll need to understand the words and concepts related to schools and education.

In their daily communication, teachers naturally use language that is familiar and intrinsically understood. They also miscommunicate, though, and communication suffers most when it deals with trends that come and go.

Teachers constantly participate in conversations with one another, to help them clarify concepts related to what happens in schools. You don't necessarily have that luxury. There's no way I can know, for example, how your particular school describes certain ideas, like 'reader'; therefore, it's impossible for me to provide every piece of information you need.

I encourage you to practise notetaking and marking up while reading this book. You can then apply this tool to newsletters, newspaper articles, report cards, websites and anything else related to your children's education.

As for the glossary, apply my definitions, add to them and use them as a guide when reading school communications or speaking with teachers.

It doesn't matter what you already know or what you don't. What matters is that you can actively participate in conversations and have the confidence to seek clarity on concepts you don't fully understand.

Promise me you won't be afraid to ask for clarity if you need it. The more you do this, the more confident you will become in all your interactions regarding your children's education.

Be honest. Be frank. Don't sugar coat!

Homework

NOW FOR YOUR HOMEWORK

If you haven't already done so, you might like to underline or highlight some points, or jot down a few notes, ready for your APLL time.

You might also like to skim over your school's website and ask yourself these questions:

1. Are there any words or concepts that are unclear?
2. Is there evidence that a 'shared language of agreement' might be worthy of further reflection?
3. Are there any confusing concepts?

It would also be worth noting the way relationships are described:

1. Is the word 'partnership' used more than the word 'relationship'?
2. What does the school say about responsibilities?
3. What do *you* think about the way in which relationships or partnerships are described?

You might like to have a 'schoolbook' specifically for homework and your APLL group meetings.

I started with a journal that very quickly became a storage space for all sorts of communication. Having one schoolbook made planning, school communication, letter writing and chatting with other parents so much easier.

Family Time

NOW THAT'S A GOOD IDEA

When your children bring home a challenging word or concept that came up in a conversation at school:

1. Start a conversation with your child

2. Get clarity on what your child understands it to mean

3. Explain any differences between people's definitions or descriptions

4. Keep a record and be sure to include the date

5. A T-Chart like the one below is one way of recording ideas.

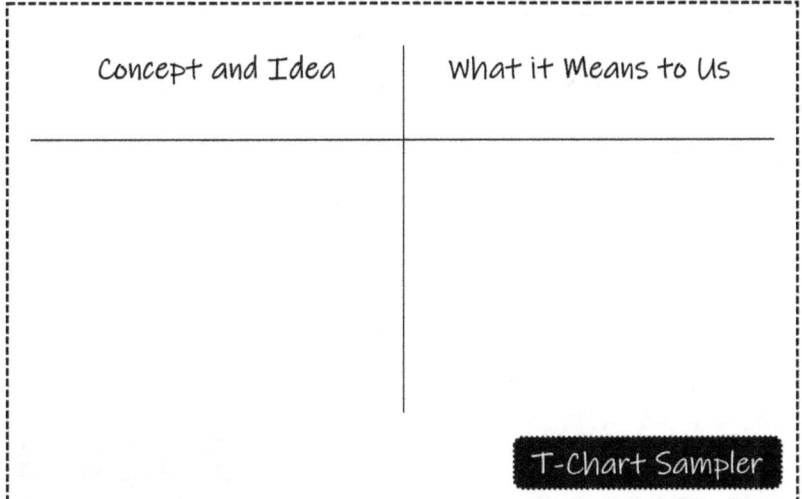

It can be a handy reference if you need to communicate with teachers or educational leaders about misunderstandings or anything else that comes up as a result.

And it can be fun to look back on, as your children grow up.

APLL Group

APLL START UP

Now's the time to plan an APLL event.

You're bringing together parents from your children's school to address the topic: *My children. Their Education. My Responsibility.*

With this book under your arm, you can open the conversation with something you've read so far.

As the conversation continues, you'll begin to find points of interest and concepts that need clarity.

The importance of 'A Shared Language of Agreement' will begin to unfold.

Step 1: Make a list of 10–15 school parents
Step 2: Pick a convenient meeting place
Step 3: Choose a date and time that allow for maximum flexibility
Step 4: Invite parents
Step 5: Remember to ask for an RSVP

APLL Start Up

These meet ups can become regular events with a new school education topic to discuss each time. You never know, your successful start-up might be enough to establish an APLL group: an independent group that doesn't require a constitution, funding or formal reporting processes.

Your chats will provide support that parents will welcome and your confidence will soar.

Learning a Shared Language of Agreement

A group of school principals I was coaching were keen to learn what could be done differently, to maximise face-to-face, one-to-one teaching time. The 'Purpose Driven Review' (PDR) I developed identified time management and communication as the two significant issues in every school. We began the change process by restoring, reducing and replacing various tactics. Over three months, the benefits were significant.

In terms of classroom practice, teachers wanted to see how they could continue to use their approaches to teaching while incorporating the proposed changes.

I agreed to do a demonstration lesson and have it recorded for use in further professional learning and evaluation. Twenty-seven principals and teachers stood around the perimeter of the classroom as I launched into a 40-minute lesson. The goal was to demonstrate how, in that time frame, all my time would be spent teaching. I planned to show nine different strategies to achieve this.

The session went according to plan and the outcomes were as anticipated. Toward the end of the lesson, I decided to throw in a curve ball. I asked a group of students to put their rubbish in the bin. No-one moved. I asked again... still nothing.

At that moment, one of the principals said, 'Students, I think Ms Lacey would like you to put your trash in the can'. Clearly, the meaning of words used by an Aussie in a room full of American educators couldn't be taken for granted.

It was a great end to an already successful session. Not only were time management and face-to-face one-on-one teaching achieved, but the principle of 'a shared language of agreement' was demonstrated in real time and became a real learning experience.

Wrap Up

- **LESSON 1:** A shared language of agreement is critical for having clarity, talking things through and getting things done.

LESSON 2:
School Education: What's the Purpose?

A quick history lesson! Schools have been around for centuries. It seems the first school was started back in 459 BC by a Jewish scribe. His aim was to provide education for fatherless boys.

Schools have been set up in monasteries and churches, in tents and even on town squares, where townsfolk would gather to read or listen. There were times when anyone could open a school and offer a curriculum. Parents would then have a choice about what their children learned and how families would spend money on education.

In more recent times, Victoria, Australia, became one of the first places in the world to introduce free, compulsory and secular education. The idea was for communities to establish committees to run their own local schools.

An *agreed non-negotiable and measurable specified curriculum* would be available to every child. It would be compulsory for children aged between 6 and 15 to attend unless they were receiving instruction from home or a church school. And, if they reached the agreed standard in the reading, writing and arithmetic curriculum before the age of 15, they no longer had to attend.

They could contribute to family life and, when they were old enough to work, they could make a valuable contribution to their growing community. Some could even continue learning if they showed sufficient ability. Scholarships were available for families without the means to pay for further education.

THE BEST OF INTENTIONS

Exploring history helps us understand how past decisions have influenced how we live today. The more we know, the better equipped we are to appreciate the intentions behind important ideas and expectations. Raising relevant questions holds greater value, too, especially if we're seeking change.

The short history of schools you've just read is full of ideas and values held generations ago. You've more than likely identified many.

Here's a list, as a guide.

- One parent families
- School facilities
- Parental choice
- Payment for education
- Free, compulsory, secular education
- Community operated local schools
- School attendance
- Agreed specified curriculum for every child
- Agreed standard of attainment
- Further education
- Scholarships.

These ideas will be explored in future lessons. Right now, there's something missing from this list that needs to be clarified: finding a school's purpose.

FINDING A SCHOOL'S PURPOSE

There's a reason or purpose behind all our actions and interactions. We're designed to interact and, when we do, we change. You know *schools are places of learning* and that education is the *action of teaching and learning.* It's fair to say that school is jam packed with action and interaction.

The concept of *life-long learning* might also be familiar. It has become the generally accepted way to explain the conceptual link between education and life.

You could say life and education have the same purpose: *to change people through teaching and learning or to take people from the unknown to the known.*

Some, but not all, of our education takes place at school.

Think about how many interactions you've had with your children over the last 7 days. What have you taught them? What have you learned from them? How about everyone else your children have interacted with? Sports coaches and teammates, faith groups, neighbours, extended family and strangers are just some who contribute to your children's education.

Chances are you're now wondering, 'If education takes place everywhere, all the time, why do we still bother with schools? What's their purpose?'

These aren't silly questions.

Neither is this statement: 'I just want my children to be happy'. It's a very real emotional desire that you and I, and most parents, share.

The logic behind this desire includes trusting that your children will take responsibility for their lives, participate in paid work, pursue personal interests and contribute responsibly to the lives of others.

The purpose of school education is just as logical.

The purpose of school education is to help you prepare your children to live a happy and responsible life.

While at school your children should learn:

1. To behave and be treated fairly
2. Essential skills and knowledge, to enable them to contribute responsibly to their own lives and the lives of others
3. How to build on those essential skills and knowledge to pursue their personal goals.

Reading this list a few times over, you'll see some values stand out: fairness, belonging, responsibility and freedom. Do you agree?

These are all characteristics of healthy families and thriving communities, which have been passed on from generation to generation.

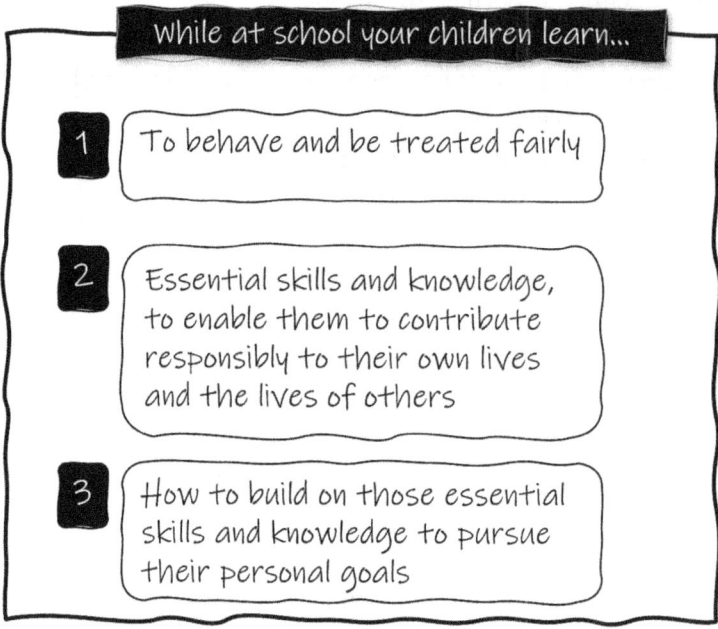

We'll continue to examine these. First, though, we'll look at the purpose of school education from another vantage point.

FOUR APPLICATIONS OF CAPABILITY

As your children learn and grow and move from school life to their working life, what they do for work and leisure will probably fall into one or more of these four areas: craft, skill, trade and profession.

1. Craft
To have a craft generally means being able to do something well, using your hands. A good example is cake decorating or pottery.

2. Skill
A skill is the result of learned and repeated efforts to carry out complex tasks. A good example is the ability to read.

3. Trade
A trade requires special training in manual work. A good example is plumbing.

4. Profession
A profession requires mastery of complex knowledge and skills, through study and practical experience over time. A good example is law.

Just how far individuals take these is a matter of personal choice.

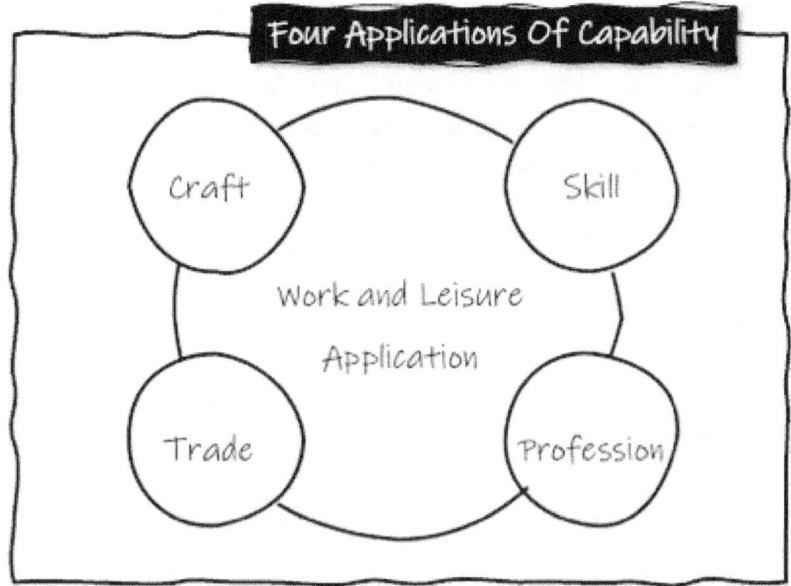

Although these four are unique. Fundamental skills and knowledge apply to all of them. Likewise, most, if not all communities, require the application of these different capabilities to function well and provide the range of services and opportunities families might need. And, chances are, your school community is representative of all four among parents, staff and students.

Homework

YESTERDAY. TODAY. TOMORROW

If you've been a collector of items related to your own childhood – especially to your schooldays – fish them out and take a look. School report cards, exercise books, essays or assignments are a good start.

Add your children's report cards and work samples to your collection. And if by chance you can get your hands on anything from your parent's school days, throw them in the mix too. You now have samples of school education from one extended family over three generations.

What's the same? How are things different? Can you see consistency in the purpose of school education?

Pop your insights into your 'schoolbook'.

Family Time

THE LADDER OF INFLUENCE

Some, but not all, of our education takes place at school. Where are the other places and who are the people who influence your family's education?

Here are six groups of possibilities.

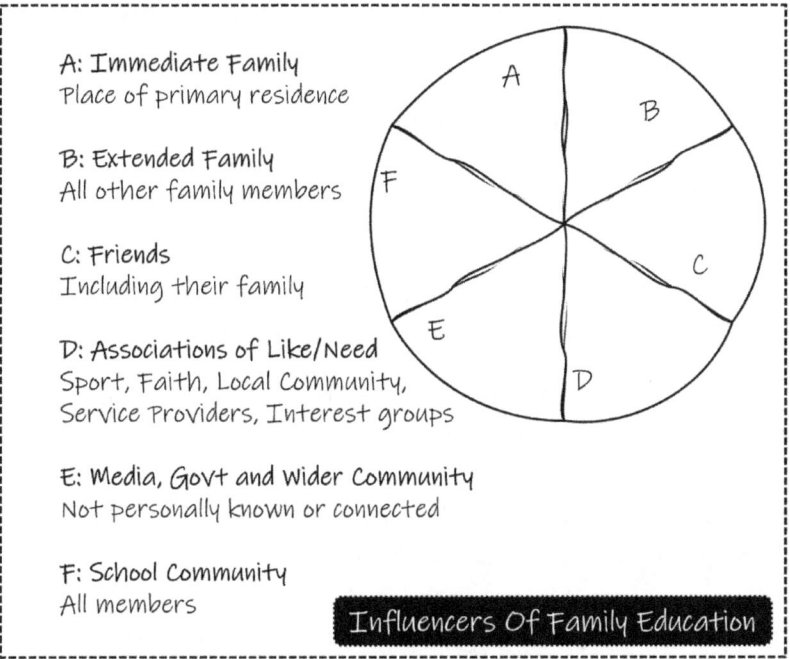

Have a conversation with your family about the six groups. Talk about what you learn from each one. You might also talk about personal goals you have about what you'd like these groups to teach you in the future.

Another interesting possibility is to see if you all agree on these six groups. Should there be more on the list? Or fewer? Or is it just right?

To finish off, share what you've read and your own thoughts about the purpose of school education. Does your family agree?

APLL Group

THE FUNDAMENTALS OF CAPABILITY

A quick reminder: The purpose of schools is to *help you* prepare your children to live a happy and responsible life.

You'll need Post-it notes for this experience.

1. Take turns to share some of your children's interests outside of school. Responses might include sport, collectables, physical activities, arts and crafts, specialist classes or tutoring.

2. Record each interest on a separate Post-it note.

3. Once everyone has contributed write 'yes' on a new Post-it, 'no' on another, and 'not sure' on another.

4. Sort the interests according to whether the school has taught fundamental capabilities that contribute to each interest. Pop each Post-it under 'yes', 'no' or 'maybe'.

5. As you're going through the interests, you're starting to build an agreed understanding of the purpose and value of school education.

When the point of view of other parents is not the same as yours, encourage healthy debate by starting with, 'I find myself disagreeing with you on…. Here's why….'

We won't always agree. We can, however, all agree to find a mutually beneficial way forward.

The goal here is to enjoy debating on what schools teach for every interest and what's not taught at school.

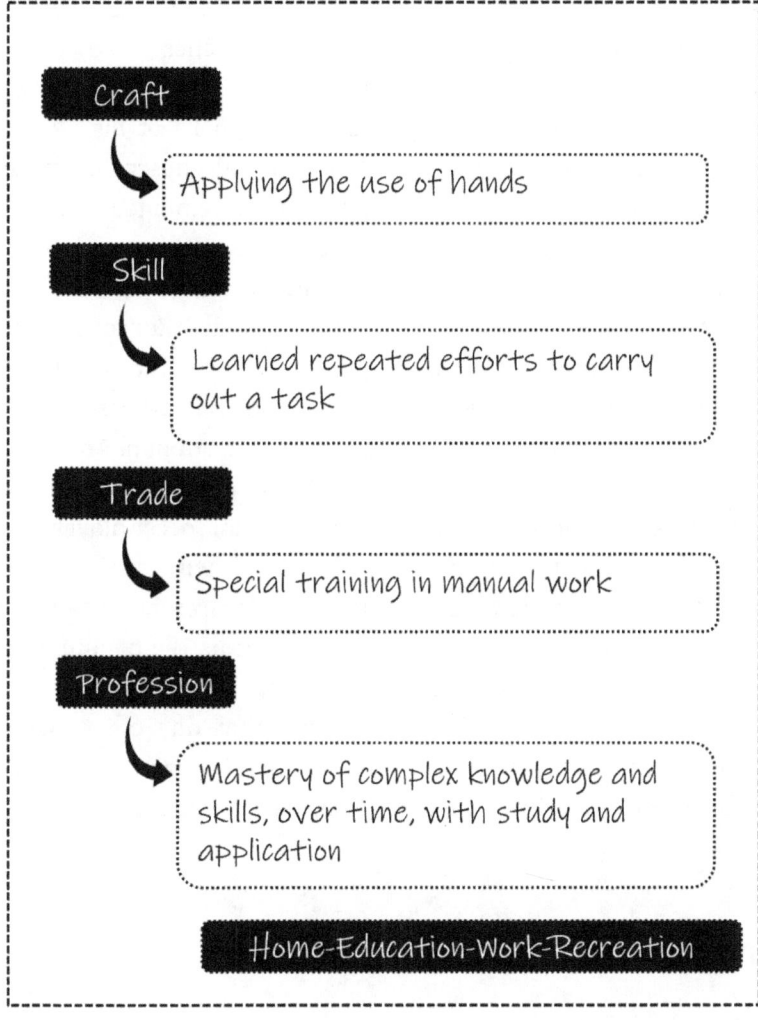

My All-Time Favourite Teacher

Some of us were blessed in our early years with a life lesson that greatly influenced our professional and personal lives. That's what happened to me at the age of 9 – it just took me a while to realise it. Learning the purpose of school education came from an unexpected event; it wasn't part of the curriculum.

Here's what happened.

My Grade 4 teacher was my all-time favourite. He was smart, funny, fair, considerate and, most important of all, strict. The expectations he had for all his students were unmistakably high.

One winter day, after we'd all marched into class after lunch, Kon was asked to join our teacher on the platform. Kon was a 'New Australian' pupil; he and his family had recently arrived from Greece. He soon became the class risk taker.

On this day, Kon had been caught smoking behind the school incinerator – clearly against school rules. He walked slowly up to the platform. Our teacher quietly assured Kon he was a valued member of the class and the entire school. He spoke of his deep disappointment that Kon had chosen to smoke on the school grounds and reminded him of his responsibility to learn, to work hard and to set an example for his classmates.

He reminded Kon of his soccer skills, suggesting Kon was the best player in the entire school and that others might do well if they could learn from him. And, with more practice and the right attitude, Kon might even become a professional soccer player.

I had just witnessed a master professional at work. Mr Uren had powerfully and respectfully taught us the genuine purpose of school education.

From that day on, Kon was no longer a smoker and I became a determined observer of teacher professionalism.

Wrap Up

- **LESSON 2:** The purpose of schools is to *help you* prepare your children to live a happy and responsible life.

LESSON 3:
Families, Fairness and Difference

It doesn't matter where you live, which school your children attend or what your family composition is; your family and every other family belong in the school community and should benefit from school education.

It doesn't matter what the make-up of each family is: some might be unique because of cultural or religious beliefs; some might be nuclear families; others might be step-families or have same-sex or single parents; some might have needed medical intervention to become a family.

Your family grouping is your own. It might even change several times during your children's school life. That's your business. Schools mustn't be influenced by this. They must provide the same basic service to every family, regardless of its composition.

This is where things can become a little bit tricky, though.

If family groupings have different composition, home languages, religious or spiritual beliefs and different financial or employment status, do these differences influence school education? Can the provision of school education for all families ever be fair? To be honest, the answer to these two questions is both yes, and no.

PARENTS AND TEACHERS; FAMILIES AND SCHOOLS

Q: Why is an elephant?

A: Because one leg is both the same.

Have you ever read anything so ridiculous? The point about this joke is twofold: first, that no question is a silly one; second, that not everything makes sense. The same can be said about parent-teacher relationships and family-school relationships.

It makes sense to send your children to school with certain expectations, especially now that your knowledge about school education is evolving. What doesn't make sense is that your expectations, the school's expectations and those of other parents aren't always the same; fairness, however, is the goal. It's often a case of 'one leg is both the same'.

You might be seen as a *helicopter parent*. Everything you do and ask is viewed by others as 'hovering' – wanting to know everything that's going on, keen to know everyone's business and determined to make sure your children don't miss out on anything.

This couldn't be further from the truth. You're genuinely interested in your children's education and like to play an active part in their lives. You take your role as a school parent very seriously. It could be said that you're a classic *Australian Parent Leading Learning*.

You could be judged an *absent parent*. You're accused of being uninterested. The truth is you simply don't have the luxury of time to be quite so involved *at* school. Your responsibility is most evident after school hours. You don't owe anyone an explanation.

If you're a parent and also a teacher who works in your children's school, what happens to your expectations? Chances are you're either the most popular among parents or the most judged. Juggling your responsibilities as a parent and as an educator could well be an ongoing challenge.

FAMILY COMPOSITION

Let's take things one step further. My family is one that has changed over time. It now consists of me and my two girls. My de facto husband has three adult children. We haven't had biological or adopted children together, so we are not a blended family.

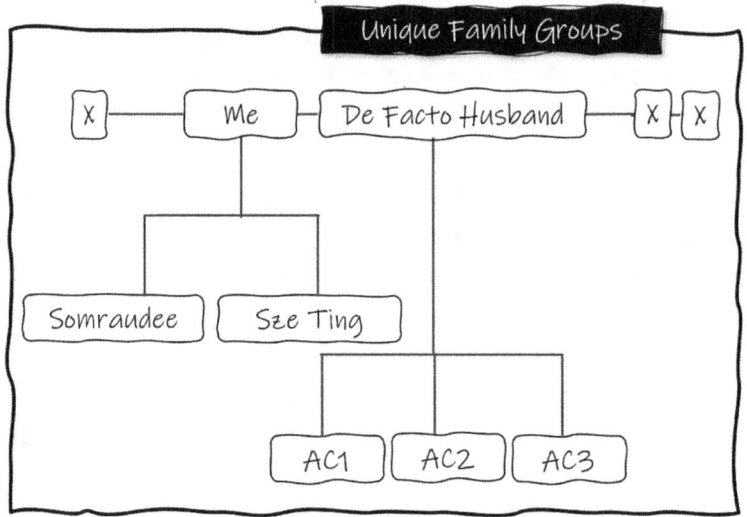

What does your family consist of?

Regardless of the composition of your family or of any other, all families share one essential characteristic. Every child was born to one biological male and one biological female. *This makes us all fundamentally equal.*

Ask yourself this question: 'Would it be fair for a child to miss out on school because of the loss of one parent and the resulting poor economic situation of the living parent?' My hunch is you would answer, 'No'. I agree; it most certainly wouldn't. Substitute this example with any family grouping and you'd give the same answer.

I hope that equality of opportunity, belonging, responsibility and what is fair in school education might be starting to make more sense.

SAME EDUCATION, DIFFERENT NEEDS

Here's another scenario. Your school has just welcomed a refugee family. The family doesn't have a strong command of English and the children have experienced trauma. There's also a lack of trust in authority and the children aren't familiar with the *rules* or *functions* of school.

In fairness, these children have the right to the same education as your children and every other child at the school. However, their genuine needs differ from the needs of your children and others at the school.

You know that the school's role is to teach an agreed curriculum, but what exactly does that look like? To what degree is the school responsible for ensuring all the needs of all children from all different families are met?

This is the challenge schools face. What is 'fair' in the provision of instruction?

You have five responsibilities here:

1. Learn all you can about the curriculum on offer for your child
2. Learn about your children's educational needs and secure agreement on those for which the school is responsible and those for which it is not
3. Seek assistance from other service providers to meet any needs the school is not qualified to meet
4. Ensure your children's needs do not adversely compromise the instruction of other children
5. Speak out if the needs of other children are adversely affecting the instruction your children are receiving.

It doesn't help anyone to assume your children's school can serve *all* families in *all* areas of need.

IT'S NOT FAIR

You've just explored the essentials in **Families, Fairness and Difference**. Fairness will continue to pop up throughout this book, just as it does in school and in the community.

Isn't it terrific that you also know how important the principle of a 'shared language of agreement' is in any communication. From now on, every time you hear or read about 'fairness' in school settings, you'll be right on topic.

You won't go down the divisive path of political correctness. You'll be frank in your conversations, you'll lead with the knowledge that you are responsible for your children and you won't be afraid to assert this.

What a positive way to bring belonging and fairness together.

Homework

WHAT'S FAIR AND HOW CAN YOU ACHIEVE IT?

No two families are the same. No two children are the same. No two schools are the same.

How can you be sure that the education your children receive at school will give them an equal opportunity in life? Does fairness in education mean the same thing for every family?

Your homework is to give these questions some thought. Jot down a few notes in the margin or in your schoolbook. We're putting together all the pieces of the school education puzzle. What's 'fair' is an important principle and one to keep thinking and learning about.

---

1. Fairness to me means...
2. Fairness at the school means...
3. We think differently about fairness because...
4. Being fair is challenging because...
5. I manage issues of fairness by...

Being Fair

Family Time

FAMILY GROUPINGS

Have a conversation with your children about your family. You might like to follow these steps:

1. Start with your immediate family: you, your children and their other parent
2. Sketch a family tree together; you might like to use the sample genogram (below) as a guide
3. Talk about members of your extended family: parents, grandparents, aunts, uncles and cousins.
4. Share stories of historical events involving family members
5. Be honest in answering any questions about family composition that might arise.

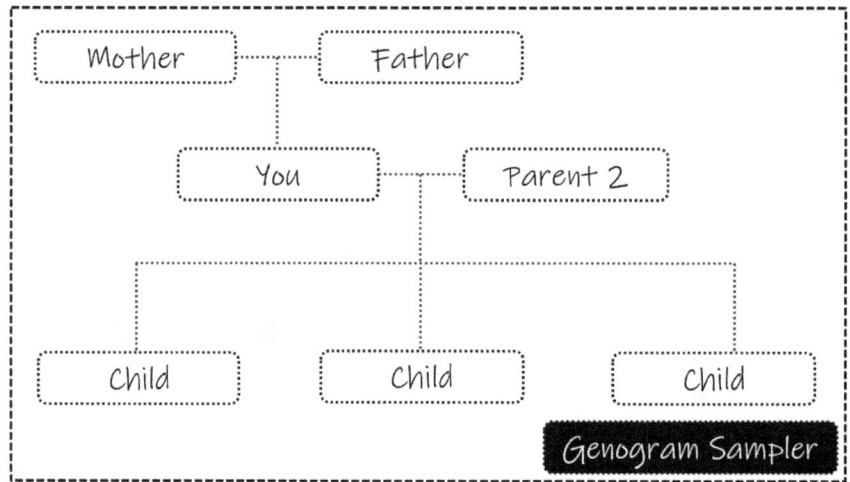

Genogram Sampler

Keep building on your family tree as changes take place and new information comes to hand. As your children mature and begin to form relationships of their own, chances are they will have a growing interest in their ancestors.

Family records are a legacy of tremendous value. Sharing your history is also a wonderful way of learning about history and how to do research. Enjoy!

APLL Group

PARENT EXPECTATIONS OF SCHOOL

What are your expectations of school education?

This is an exercise that your parent group can do to help determine how the things that happen in schools meet (or fail to meet) those expectations.

1. List all things your children are involved in at school
2. Create a three-column chart like the one below.

Needs	Wants	Maybe

Needs, Wants, Maybe

3. Transfer your list to the chart, according to whether the items are about needs or wants, or you're not really sure
4. Now add to the chart any other expectations you have
5. Compare your chart with those of other parents in the group
6. Try to create a 'master chart' that combines the items on individual charts.

Comparing charts and resolving differences between what's in the master chart and what's really happening in the school is a really powerful way to explore values and what everyone thinks is essential.

If your APLL group has members from different schools, including public, private and denominational, comparisons between them will be very interesting.

If your group doesn't include this range, it might be worth considering. There are sure to be parents with friends and siblings with children of school age who might be interested in joining you every now and then.

Becoming Family

When Somraudee was in primary school, she was interviewed for a teaching publication. She talked openly about what it was like to grow up as an adopted child. Here's the interview:

What is adoption?
It is when the parents that gave birth to you decide that either they can't look after you, don't want to look after you, or know there are better parents out there for you. They choose for you to have a new opportunity.

How does intercountry adoption work?
Adults from around the world send applications to the department in their country and then the application goes to the country they want to adopt a child from. The whole process takes about five years, and the two countries work together to get the right child for the couple.

Can you share a little bit about your journey?
Well, I know a lot. Some I will keep to myself and some I will tell. I was born in Thailand and lived with foster parents before I stayed in a children's home for a little while. When I was in the children's home, I received a photo album so that I could learn a little about my new family life in Australia. When my mum arrived at the children's home we walked around for a little while and she filled in some paperwork. Then we left together. So, from that day in Krabi, she was my mum.

Do you remember much?
No, not exactly. Mum has lots of stories about it. And it's really cool because parents talk about the first things their children did like smile and crawl. But because I was nearly four, my mum talks about my first English word, which was 'shower' and how I could count to ten in English after just four days.

Are there some important phrases or things that we should know about adoption and being adopted?
When you're adopted, the family that you know you are going to spend the rest of your life with, are your family. They don't become your 'fake family', which is what some kids make the mistake of thinking. The family that you were with before you were adopted are your birth family.

Does it feel different to be adopted?
Not really. If you have been with your family for a couple of years, you start to get used to them and feel like they are actually your birth parents. I just know my mum loves me and I know she is my mum.

Do you think some of your friends are proud because they have a friend from another country and background?
I can't tell. They just treat me like everybody else.

Do you find people are curious about your family background and ask questions?
Well, I do get asked a lot of questions. When I was in Year 1 and Year 2 at school it was hard. It kind of makes you upset when kids ask, 'Who are your real parents?', because they are referring to your birth parents. You can get upset

with that because you try really hard to explain it and they don't always understand. So actually, they don't get what adoption is.

Are there any times when being adopted is difficult?
Well, not knowing my birth parents for a start. And not knowing my relatives. It's also hard when I am sometimes asked questions that are not easy for me to find words for. I get frustrated because I want people to understand, but they don't, and it is a really easy thing to understand. Well, for me it is.

So, if you could explain it to your friends and even strangers, what would you say?
We're just a normal family like yours. It's just that we had a different beginning.

Wrap Up

- **LESSON 3:** Schools must provide the same basic service to every family, regardless of its composition.

LESSON 4:
Play by the Rules

When you play a game, it's likely you know the rules before you begin. If not, you learn them quickly. Having and following rules means you have the same chance of winning as everyone else.

Your family rules are there to teach your children to live with others. They learn that when rules are broken, there are consequences. It's one way you prepare your children to live in society.

When they go to school your children learn through instruction. Schools also have rules. And, like rules of a game and rules at home, to be fair, the rules should apply to the whole school community. There are broader rules, too, that apply to the whole school system.

Laws are rules. They are there to protect and ensure our rights are not abused by other people, by organisations – including schools – and by the government. When they are broken, there are consequences. Sometimes those consequences affect others more than they affect the law breakers.

Whether they are rules of the sandpit, the playground, the classroom, the whole school or the community, rules apply to all of us, because that's how Western society works.

How well do you know the school rules? Perhaps you know them as policies.

THE RULE OF LAW

Can I suggest we go a step further and explore how school rules are linked to the rule of law in society?

Let's be clear. I'm not a lawyer. Far from it. I hadn't spent much time studying the rule of law until a situation arose where I needed to. It taught me so much more than I learned at teacher's college. Now I'm sharing with you a little of what I learned. I would never want you or any parent to experience what our family went through.

That's a story for another day. Let's keep the focus on *your* vantage point.

It's really important you understand the basics. To be honest, one of the problems we face in schools is that the rule of law has become so complex that many parents tend to throw their hands in the air when dealing with school problems. It all seems too hard and they don't know the basics.

But not you!

You're about to read up on the basics. No parent should have to be a lawyer to understand what happens in schools or have to go it alone when something isn't quite right.

DIFFERENT KINDS OF LAW

There are various kinds of law. They make up the framework for every rule in society to be created and followed. Some rules in your home and your children's school may be a little different from those of other families and the schools their children attend – like screentime or uniformas. In the end, we all live by these various kinds of law.

Notice I said, 'kinds of law'.

Take a look at this short list of scenarios:

- Your child is pushed off the play equipment and breaks a bone. Is this a school matter or a personal one between two families?
- A school bullying situation continues into the school holidays. Should you notify the school?

- You're volunteering at school and the teacher leaves the room. An accident occurs. Who is responsible – you, the school or the teacher? Who had a duty of care?

- You plan a family break during school term. Your child will be absent for 17 school days. Do you need permission from the school?

- You are dealing with a custody situation. Does the school need to know?

These are genuine situations that some parents have faced.

How would you handle each one?

Not everything that happens at home is the school's business. But everything that happens to your children at school is *your* business. Every school and school system operates inside a complex web of laws. Knowing how school rules relate to the law is also your business.

Here goes.

CONSTITUTIONAL LAW

Countries, states, companies and organisations, such as sporting clubs and schools, have governing bodies. The members of a governing body have the ultimate responsibility to make decisions that accord with the agreed basic rights that everyone within that specific organisation is entitled to. These basic rights are written in a constitution.

Every school has a leader, middle managers and a school board. Your children's school board (school council) is its governing body. The school board is responsible for making decisions about your children's school. In doing so, it must follow its own constitution. This is the set of rules that explains the power of the board and the rights of staff, students and parents.

As in any organisation, the school's constitution is strongly aligned with its community's beliefs and values. More about that shortly.

Think of the constitution as the umbrella under which all decision makers do what's right for their

community.

STATUTORY LAW

Statutory law is written law that has been debated and agreed on by government. It includes laws that clarify how the government functions and how order is maintained in business, civil and personal life.

There are thousands of laws at federal, state and local government level. In fact, there are so many it's impossible for anyone to know everything about the law. Not even the law makers themselves can know everything related to statutory law.

Here's an example: In Victoria, Australia, the first Education Act was six pages long. Today it's more than 810 pages in length. It also refers to dozens of other laws. That is how complex law has become.

It's good for you to know that every policy developed at your children's school is related to statutory law. It doesn't matter whether your children attend government, Catholic, independent or home-based schools. The rules or laws made by the Commonwealth and the relevant State Parliament relate to all schools in that state.

It's up to every school board to ensure its school rules and policies reflect statutory law. If ever you decide to serve on the school board, you'll find government departments have developed standard policies for schools to use as a guide. More about that in **Part 3: Lessons from the Boardroom**.

COMMON LAW

When someone breaks the law, the consequences might be a warning, a fine or something more serious. In severe cases, the offender might have to appear in court.

The role of the court is to compare the alleged behaviour of the offender with the expected behaviour related to the law that has been broken. The decision is made by referring to common law – a collection of decisions made in the past. Over time, these decisions determine the standard punishment that is usually applied.

The same applies in schools. There is a set of expected behaviours right across the school, regardless of the classroom your children are in or the teachers they have. Consequences or punishments for behaviours that go against these expectations should be consistent.

WHY THE LAW?

Part of me wants to apologise for dragging you through this lesson on law and order. To be honest, the other part of me knows better.

You need to know and understand these basic principles of law. They influence how you live, work, play, raise your children and advocate for your children's education.

Without this starting point, you have no way of knowing whether or not the government, the bureaucracy, or your children's school is behaving properly, lawfully or ethically. And, without this basic knowledge, you have no chance of doing anything about it if they're not.

You are responsible for your family, your children's education and your future.

School rules are about law and order. Everything that happens in schools is connected to a rule of law – whether it is following a rule or breaking one.

School rules must be fair and everyone in your school community must respect and apply the rule of law.

BELIEFS AND VALUES

As well as following laws, you and your family also live and act in accordance with a set of beliefs and values that are important to you. Schools do the same. Ideally there is synergy between the two, which strengthens family-school connections.

Outside the home and school bubble, as well as laws there is a set of core beliefs that more broadly guide our democracy and how we live. These beliefs have their origins in the Judaeo-Christian tradition.

This doesn't mean you have to be or become Christian. All members of society can still have their own religious beliefs. What it means, though, is that to be fair in law, the key principles of this tradition, on which our society was built, apply to everyone. This is a good thing.

An example is the principle of 'innocent until proven guilty'.

Imagine your children were accused of something they didn't do, and the word of the accuser went unchallenged. That's not how you'd want things to be. You'd want to advocate for your children, wouldn't you? Even if it turned out your child *had* broken the rules, you would want him or her to have the benefit of the doubt until it were proved.

The principle of 'innocent until proven guilty' might not be expressed in exactly that way at your children's school, but it should be implied and applied. The principle covers situations where there has been an alleged wrong done by teachers, support staff, the principal or the school board, not just by children or their parents.

To understand how the Judaeo-Christian tradition informs our society, do a little research on the Ten Commandments.

Homework

THE RULES OF SCHOOL

Time to start navigating your way around the school. And I don't mean on foot. You're going to do a little research for yourself and in preparation for your next gathering of APLL.

Your school will probably fall into one of two categories:

1. Document Savvy
2. Document Sloppy

The Document Savvy School

This type of school will have a policy on absolutely everything related to school. There will also be loads of other documents, including tip sheets, promotional flyers, newsletters, ezines… the list goes on. Everything will be up to date and up to the minute in terms of presentation, style, and readily available in a parent handbook or online.

The Document Sloppy School

In this school, there will be just a smattering of documents and policies – many incomplete or out of date, if they exist at all.

Go fossicking. Check online, go to the office, chat to the teachers and find out what's available and where to find it. You'll be surprised what you might learn.

Family Time

CONVERSATIONS AND COMMANDMENTS

What better way to spend family time than to have real conversations.
Sit together at the dinner table and chat over your evening meal.
If you're not doing this already, make every effort to do so as often as possible.

A regular conversation shared around the dinner table with my girls centred on problem solving. For example: 'I had a problem. Here's how I fixed it'; or 'I have a problem. I've done my best to fix it and now I need some help'.

Learning about the Ten Commandments is another way to develop meaningful conversations.

Try this for starters:

Step 1: Read the Ten Commandments

Step 2: Pick one to talk about

Step 3: Talk about whether or not it matches your family's beliefs

Step 4: Agree on what to do if there is disagreement.

Here is an adaptation of the Ten Commandments, respectfully written as an introduction for young learners. They are in no particular order and other versions are available.

1. Put God First
2. Stay away from fake Gods
3. Don't misuse God's name
4. Make Sunday a day of rest
5. Love and respect your mum and dad
6. Never hurt anyone
7. Keep wedding promises
8. Don't take anything that isn't yours
9. Always tell the truth
10. Do not wish for other people's things

The 10 Commandments

APLL Group

LOCAL PARENT SUPPORT

A wish I have for you is that your APLL group will become a regular feature of your life as a school parent. Taking the lead will be so much more enjoyable and less stressful if others are travelling the same road with you. A simple strategy to help you get started is coming up next.

Get to know the school better by getting to know parents better. Once the school bell rings, you'll be spending more time with school parents and their children. There'll be birthday parties, play dates, school holidays and, possibly, strong friendships for many years to come.

Doesn't it make sense that this should become your support base? The more you come together as parents, the stronger your voice and the greater your chance of being number one in your children's school education.

I realise you might be thinking I'm repeating myself but trust me. If you share your understanding of school education and your questions about it, you'll soon let go of anything that's preventing you from having your children's back.

From this point on, expect more reminders to meet as a group of Australian Parents Leading Learning.

Here are few tips to boost support for one another:

> 1. Your children's safety and their education are priorities
> 2. Help each other prevent politically motivated division from affecting your APLL group
> 3. Meet in person as much as possible
> 4. Learn about each other's experiences of school
> 5. Agree on two ways of information sharing: topics to share with and beyond your group; personal information confidential to your group only
> 6. Promote your APLL group
> 7. Be proud of representing your children and helping other parents do the same
> 8. Have a process for communicating with parents who can and cannot meet in person.
>
> **APLL Tips**

Traffic Lights

I made my first trip to Morocco during the mid 90s. The Marrakech medina, the markets and the snake charmers, the Atlas Mountains, riding camels and sleeping out in the desert were all highlights.

Fes was charming too, with its narrow alleys, medieval architecture and ornate tile works.

Casablanca sounded romantic, probably because of the movie with the same name. I was so looking forward to exploring the city.

To my shock and horror, people in motor vehicles and even those with donkeys paid no attention to the traffic lights in the city centre. It was a case of every man – and donkey – for himself. There was horn honking, road rage and total confusion everywhere and everyone's safety was at risk.

It was an experience to talk and laugh about later but also a firm reminder of why every society and community must live by agreed and established rules.

Wrap Up

- **LESSON 4:** The rule of law is represented in schools through rules and policies that must be agreed to and understood by everyone in the community.

LESSON 5:
Home Life at School

You're at the school gates and you tell your children to have a great day. You wave them goodbye as you jump in the car and head off for another busy day. Who's responsible for your children once you've gone? And what exactly does that responsibility involve?

You know you are responsible for raising your children and you have a right and a duty to fulfil that responsibility. That's the law.

You also know that help is at hand, including in the area of education. You gratefully accept that assistance. Do you know, however, precisely what that family/school relationship means when you're not there?

Schools aren't what they were 30, 40 or 50 years ago. The chance of your children having male teachers, for example, is pretty slim. Students no longer march into school after singing the national anthem (maybe this needs a comeback) and the Australian flag is now just one among many. The traditional role of stay-at-home parents isn't as common as it once was, either. Parents work long hours and schools are more involved in family matters than ever before.

Expectations you have at home might or might not match those of the school. And, when they don't,

to what extent can principals and teachers step in on your behalf – especially when families are so varied and when many teachers are also parents. This can be a vexing issue and not an easy one to resolve.

DUTY OF CARE

Schools have a duty of care. *They have an obligation to avoid acting or failing to act in a way they know could injure or harm others.* Principals and teachers have a duty of care to your children. They must not delegate their duty of care to anyone else.

Obvious measures school staff take to prevent harm include keeping the school premises safe and making sure children are adequately supervised.

Although these measures make sense, there are many occasions when a school's duty of care is unclear.

Let's say you don't feed your children breakfast and you fail to provide a school lunch. Does the school have a duty to feed your children? If you have failed in your own duty to your children, to what degree should the school step in? I know this won't happen to you, but it's an example of the broader problems schools face.

Another problem is how to reconcile different recollections when an incident has occurred or when a lack of clarity compromises someone's position.

You'll find reference to 'duty of care' in the school policies, consent forms and school education websites. There could even be a statement like this: 'Teachers stand in the place of parents' or 'Parents see their children as consumers with contractual rights'.

What you won't find is an open acknowledgement that your responsibility as a parent for your children is greater than the authority of school staff.

It's a murky area and can become rather complicated.

A *duty of care* is everyone's responsibility.

STUDENT AGENCY AND INFORMED CONSENT

You might be familiar with the concepts of *self-directed* and *child-centred* learning. They're philosophies that focus on giving children greater influence and decision making about what and how they learn.

Student agency is another concept many schools are introducing. This is based on a belief that students have the ability and the will to influence their own lives.

Although you should encourage your children to be responsible for their learning, a cause for concern is that these philosophies can reduce your input into your children's education.

NATURAL AND COMPLEX FAMILY MATTERS

Schools are witness to the natural cycle of family life. Children welcome new siblings, participate in many celebrations, experience illness and the death of loved ones. Families might go through separation and divorce.

Some families experience more difficult and complex matters.

Are you familiar with the term 'parentectomy'?

Let's apply this definition: Parentectomy is a colloquial word for the removal of parental contact with children, or the removal of a parent's power of decision making with regard to their children. This can apply to one or both parents.

Parents themselves can carry out a 'parentectomy', when one parents turns the children against the other parent.

Of great concern is that it's also common in medical settings and in schools. Doctors and teachers have been known to make decisions about children's health or education without parents' input or knowledge.

It seems that some believe your *right to be a responsible parent* has no value.

This is an extreme example of a complex family matter.

MATURE MINORS

Many schools have also introduced wellbeing programs, and teachers in these roles have varying degrees of capability and life experience. A 'wellbeing teacher' is there to support students in developing self-management strategies for issues ranging from study techniques to anxiety and mental health problems and relationship issues. Personal family matters can also come into play.

Here's the catch. Your children are children until the age of 18. You are still required to sign permission forms, sometimes right up to the time your children are 18. With regard to some matters, however, some schools choose not to obtain your permission. Instead, they grant children permission to make their own decisions. The principal or other staff given the authority can consider them to be *mature minors*.

The law recognises no specific age when a young person may be sufficiently mature and capable of making their own decision. Still, the law recognises some children under 18 can decide about various issues, including their education, healthcare and well-being. These young people are referred to as 'mature minors'.

This means school staff can help your children make life changing decisions *without your consent.*

There is an assumption that these children – or mature minors – are in full knowledge of the possible consequences of the decisions they make. It's a contentious issue.

If schools assume a duty of care, yet provide room for children to make their own decisions, where does this leave you and your responsibility to, and for, your children?

What might be the impact on your family, and others, if you're dealing with sensitive family matters?

At best, school employees would refer your child to other service providers with expertise in complex matters. At worst they could help your children remove you from their lives.

RESPONSIBLE AND FAIR ADULT INTERACTION

A child's level of innocence or maturity isn't the same in all situations, and every child is different.

Some concepts require greater levels of maturity to comprehend and take responsibility for. Not everyone agrees what these levels are or how to achieve them.

Perhaps, a shared language of agreement about the terms *student* and *child* is a worthy beginning. This is an important principle: 'student' and 'child' are not the same. Other terms on which it's important to have agreement are 'principal', 'parent' and 'guardian'. The same principle could apply to the last two: 'parent' and 'guardian' are not the same.

Why not make an appointment with your school principal to learn more about *duty of care*, *mature minors* and other terms and how they are applied in your children's school setting?

When you do, follow this rule of thumb: never meet with the principal on your own. Always have a support person with you and suggest that the principal does the same. It helps keep expectations tangible and avoids misunderstanding.

Come to think of it, there's something else you can do right now. Talk it over with your APLL group and agree about requesting an information evening on the topic. After all, duty of care is everyone's responsibility and everyone is affected when authority becomes murky. Who has greater authority over your child at school - you or the principal?

Here's how you might go about it:

1. Gather support from at least 3 other parents, preferably from different year levels. Perhaps some in your APLL group will volunteer to enlist new parents in this case

2. If your school has a *Parents and Friends Association,* approach this group in the first instance. They might be able to continue the process on your behalf. Otherwise, obtain contact details for your school board president

3. Write a friendly letter to the president, requesting an information evening

4. Be prepared to assist, as requested – even if that means delegating tasks to other parents.

Make sure there's time allowed for a Q&A. It's a great way to build relationships and encourage respectful conversations about parent, student and school responsibilities.

The information evening should also include conversations about how parents can help their children take ownership for their learning. You can't learn for them, but you can certainly teach them to become more responsible over time.

GOOD QUESTION

Concepts aren't always easy to grasp and, sometimes, difficult concepts that arise in classrooms, playground chatter and playdates can present challenges. Your children are learning as they grow. So are you.

Let's say your children are 9 and 12 years of age. You're well practised in bringing up the 9-year-old, as it's your second time around. You're also doing pretty well with the 12-year-old. But raising a 16-year-old? Right now, you've got no idea. You're going to have to wait a few more years.

Like you, I'm going through the same thing. Perhaps having to teach Somraudee English had something to do with it but I quickly worked out a way to manage the challenging concepts that can come up in conversation.

My method might be useful for you too. It's goes something like this: 'That's a really good question. It's a question a 13-year-old would ask. When you're 13, remind me and we'll talk about it then.'

This response works very well. You acknowledge your children's curiosity, honour their right to learn but avoid exposing them further to concepts that are beyond their maturity level.

Oh, and one other thing. When working with teachers I often ask this question: 'Is your position on this matter a personal or professional one?' Don't hesitate to ask this of your children's teachers if you have to approach them concerning information or opinions you don't feel are appropriate for your children's age or for discussing in the classroom.

The teacher's response will give you an indication of how to manage this and other situations – including taking the matter further.

THEY'RE YOUR CHILDREN

Your family, and many others, belong to your children's school community. Many also belong to faith groups, local businesses, clubs and other organisations.

Questions related to families are often raised in schools. They might come up in a topic for study, in a conversation about a book read, because of a social issue being discussed or in the playground.

Your expectations regarding responsible conversations might be different from the school's expectations or those of other families.

You'd be wise to make sure your children know how to answer questions that might come up, including how to describe your family unit and, especially, regarding sensitive matters.

This couldn't be more important in schools today. The respect once given equally to all children is being compromised by political correctness – and apparently without consequences.

There's a lesson here.

What your family shares, and with whom you share it is a decision for your family alone. It is for you to decide what is said, what is shared and what remains private about your family composition and family life.

Don't be fooled into believing that it's the schools business. It isn't. There's a difference between providing essential information for enrolment, emergencies and educational purposes and revealing more private details.

Here's a personal explanation of how I see the difference.

Somraudee and Ting's godmother, Maree, and her husband, Albert, were on Malaysian Airlines Flight MH17 that was shot down over the Ukraine. Somraudee and I were at home when we were given the tragic news. As soon as I could, I raced to Ting's school to inform her teacher and ask that she avoid speaking about it in class or in the staffroom until I could tell Ting the news after school. It was important for me to tell her teacher because of the public nature of our very personal loss.

On the other hand, whenever Somraudee and Ting have been absent from school for medical or family reasons and teachers have asked why, I have taught them to say, 'You'll have to speak with my mum'.

One more thing.

Don't ever assume that anything you or your children disclose will remain confidential. School staff rooms were 'social media' hubs well before Facebook and Twitter came along and very little has changed. The same can be said for playgrounds. As much as you'd like to believe otherwise, 'gossip can be gold' in schools.

You could say a family is responsible for what happens at home but everyone has a responsibility for what happens in school. After all, that's what we are: *A community of families coming together for learning and teaching.* And that includes understanding the difference between public and private matters.

Homework

PREPARING FOR PRIVACY

Think about the information you provide schools and your conversations with your children's teachers.

Depending on how long you have been a school parent, you might be surprised by how much personal information you have disclosed.

Now consider what you know and don't know about your children's teachers.

For example, if your child's teacher is absent, does a letter go home to parents explaining a doctor's appointment, the nature of a legal matter or the name of a loved one in the hospital? You know the answer to this. It's a firm 'no'.

Finally, consider respectful but firm phrases you might use when a school employee asks about, or expect to be informed about, things you consider to be private family matters.

Family Time

HIDE OR TELL (IF YOU'RE GAME)

As a bit of a play on the 'Show And Tell' theme, start your own 'Hide Or Tell' family time. It's really very simple. When a sensitive event takes place or a sensitive topic comes up, spend time talking about how much, if anything, should be shared at school. What's fair and reasonable?

> 1. Should you tell?
> 2. What would you hide?
> 3. Is it OK to tell just a little and leave other things out?
> 4. Who can you tell? Who can't you tell? Why? Why not?
> 5. What's the difference between honesty and privacy?
> 6. If you need help, who do you trust? What is it that makes you feel this way?
> 7. How might you ask for help?
>
> Hide Or Tell

I'm sure you get the idea.

While your children are young, they'll need a lot of guidance from you. As they get older, especially during puberty, some topics might be a little challenging and they might even shut down. Even so, with a history of 'Hide Or Tell' behind you, your children will know the drill.

'Hide Or Tell' is useful for defusing difficult situations and removing blame if things don't go quite right.

One other thing. 'Hide Or Tell' can be applied beyond school conversations to those with extended family, friends, other associations or clubs in which your children are involved and in managing social media.

APLL Group

GROWING UP

Distribute this to your group for pre-reading before you catch up.

Have you taught your children how to ride a bike yet? You usually begin with a tricycle, then progress to a 2-wheeler with trainer wheels. When the trainer wheels are off, there you are, running behind, hanging on to the sissy bar. You let go, just for a minute, and then grab hold again, until eventually your supporting hand is no longer needed.

At this point, your children know how to balance and brake. Their confidence is soaring.

But guess what? They're still children. You wouldn't dream of letting them jump from bicycle to motorbike.

They still have to learn how to ride over rough terrain and in poor weather. They must understand their place among other cyclists on bicycle tracks and among other commuters on roads.

From enjoying their first success on the tricycle to becoming a confident cyclist, they've come a long way. Despite these wonderful milestones, though, their vantage point is still that of a child.

Navigating the school playground and classroom is a little like learning how to ride a bicycle. Children generally play alongside classroom buddies their own age while learning to fit in among older students and adults.

In the classroom, just as on the bicycle, their focus is on the road ahead.

Now for Your Conversation Starter

As your children mature, innocence and responsibility co-exist. And, as you've read earlier in the section on 'mature minor', there's no concrete age that all children mature at the same time.

Exposure to more adult concepts, an expectation of increased responsibility or more 'adult like behaviour' happens in classrooms. It can also happen on playdates and in the playground.

You can't always control what is said by others, what your children hear, see or experience in your absence. You do, however, have an influence on how your children manage different situations and what they tell you.

Then, there's the matter of involvement. How much should school staff be involved and when do you speak with other affected parents?

This conversation will be great preparation for the Q&A session at the school information evening – if you go ahead with it.

In the meantime, here's a few tips for your APLL group as your relationships grow.

> 1. Your children's safety and their education are priorities
> 2. Help each other prevent politically motivated division from affecting your APLL group
> 3. Meet in person as much as possible
> 4. Learn about each other's experiences of school
> 5. Agree on two ways of information sharing: topics to share with and beyond your group; personal information confidential to your group only
> 6. Promote your APLL group
> 7. Be proud of representing your children and helping other parents do the same
> 8. Have a process for communicating with parents who can and cannot meet in person.
>
> **APLL Tips**

Curious Innocence About Family Life

Going through intercountry adoption generally means that your private life is no longer 'private'. Strangers ask personal questions; obvious physical differences between you and your children tend to invite inquiries.

Each time a curious stranger asked me about Somraudee, I'd politely acknowledge the question and explain it was up to my daughter to answer, if she chose to. As an adult, I could handle it; my goal was to respect her vantage point.

Over time, I taught her several ways to respond.

Most conversations were very pleasant. It was only on rare occasions that Somraudee would say, 'Thank you for asking. I don't want to answer that'. Sometimes she would say, 'You can answer, Mum'.

I've always been very proud of how well she conducted herself.

It wasn't only strangers who were curious. When Somraudee was in Year 2, she was being teased at school. One day, as I was dropping her off, a classmate came over and asked if I was Somraudee's mum.

I asked Somraudee if she wanted to answer the question. She said, 'No, mum, you can today'.

I turned to the boy and asked, 'Do you mean, am I Somraudee's real mum?'

'Yep, that's right', he said.

'Yes, I am Somraudee's real mum and Somraudee's birth mum lives in Thailand'.

He looked at the two of us and said, 'I knew that'.

Nope. He was totally confused.

Two nights later, we received news about Sze Ting. After four years, Somraudee was finally a big sister. She was beside herself with excitement and couldn't wait to share her news. She woke early the next morning and raced off to school with a photo of Sze Ting proudly tucked under her arm. I went along as a support.

Here's how it went.

Somraudee stood up for show and tell and proudly said, 'Good morning, girls and boys. I've got a new baby sister and here she is'. And, with that, she held up the photo of Sze Ting.

The boy turned immediately to me, pulled on my trouser leg and asked, 'Are you pregnant?'

Somraudee took responsibility for what she shared about her family. It put an end to the curiosity and the teasing.

Wrap Up

- **LESSON 5**: Families might see privacy and responsibility differently but agreement on these concepts is essential in schools.

LEARNINGS FROM PART 1:
Lessons From The Sandpit

LESSON 1: A shared language of agreement is critical for having clarity, talking things through and getting things done.

LESSON 2: The purpose of schools is to help you prepare your children to live a happy and responsible life.

LESSON 3: Schools must provide the same basic service to every family, regardless of its composition.

LESSON 4: The rule of law is represented in schools through rules and policies that must be agreed to and understood by everyone in the community.

LESSON 5: Families might see privacy and responsibility differently but agreement on these concepts is essential in schools.

Part 2:
Lessons From The Classroom

Lessons From The Classroom

1. Schools And The Philosophy of Education

2. Pedagogy And Personalised Learning

3. Those Who Teach

4. Curriculum Matters

5. Reading And Beyond

6. Getting Down To Basics

7. Measure That

8. School Comes At A Cost

9. Big Tech, Little Tech

10. School Days

What's your vantage point now? How does it compare with the one you had when you first started reading this book?

Such a lot has been covered in Part 1. You could say that it is basically about 'relationships'.

It explores the relationship between you and your children's other parent and the one between you and your children. It largely deals with fundamental principles about family-school relationships – between your family and the school, between you and the teachers, between your children and the teachers and the relationship you have with other parents and families.

Refer back to Part 1, when you need to, and take these key points forward:

- Raising children is an honour and a privilege; a parent's responsibility must be sincerely encouraged and never weakened. It's also the law

- For you to fulfil your right to take responsibility for raising your children, a shared language of agreement is critical

- Conversations between families and schools about school education are important; however, not all conversations about families should occur at school.

As you move into Part 2, remember to keep connecting these and other learnings. That's the nature of school education – just about everything is interconnected. Suppose you think of school education as a system. In that case, you will become more aware of one change, improvement or problem's impact on other people or situations. You could say everything that happens in or about school is about relationships.

In Part 2 you'll explore the nuts and bolts of how schools work. Each of the 10 lessons is a snapshot of the day-to-day business of school education.

Here are a few thoughts before you get started:

- Not everything you read in this section will be new to you
- Your vantage point is now one of a more informed, responsible parent
- Your APLL group will continue to be a great source of discussion, reflection and support
- Remember, if something affects you, chances are it's also affecting lots of other parents and families
- School education doesn't have to be complicated.

And remember, I won't ask anything of you I haven't learned or experienced myself. If you get stuck, write your questions in the margins, share them with other parents or ask me. I've been there, so help me to help you take the lead.

LESSON 1:
Schools and the Philosophy of Education

Have you ever caught yourself wondering something and then realising that millions of others have wondered the same thing – maybe even thousands of years ago? That's a little like how philosophy works.

Philosophy means 'love of wisdom'. It's when we seek to know ourselves and the world around us. Our curiosity then extends to our relationship with the world and with each other. It's all part of becoming 'wise'.

If you were to say we all had wisdom in varying degrees, you'd be right. Some people ask profound 'what', 'how' and 'why' questions. Others dig less deeply. Overall, though, we're all curious beings, which is good.

To have a philosophy is to have a set of principles to believe in and to live by. Fairness is one principle we've begun to explore: to be 'fair' is to behave without favouritism.

Fairness is a significant element of the beliefs and laws that guide Western society and which include the ten commandments, nations' constitutions and common law. We've looked briefly at those too.

Putting them into practice comes with enormous challenges but, without a philosophy, you're flying blind. Earlier in the book, you read about the possibility of accepting things in 'blind faith'. I'm confident your blind faith in schools is disappearing pretty quickly. That's a good thing. It's the only way to have a genuine family-school relationship.

We've also started to look more closely at the principle of free, compulsory and secular school education. In considering this, don't assume our focus is only on government schools – far from it.

'Free, compulsory and secular education' is the principle underlying a specified curriculum that includes fundamental teachings in English and Mathematics. The intention was to give every child the same chance as any other to get a basic education. It takes us back to fairness and brings us to a philosophy of education.

Being curious about school education benefits you and your curiosity includes asking questions – lots of them. After all, that's what great philosophers have always done.

WHAT'S YOUR PHILOSOPHY?

Here are two questions for you:

Question 1: What is the purpose of education?
I know you can confidently answer this. You might say:

>*The purpose of education is to change people through teaching.*

>Or

>*Education is moving from the unknown to the known.*

Question 2: What is your philosophy of education?
I'll forgive you if you can't answer this one just yet. A definition, to help you, might be:

A philosophy of education is an explanation of the values and beliefs about teaching and learning.

The truth is, very few educators can answer both questions with confidence. It's understandable. A philosophy of education explores fundamental terms and concepts, such as 'teacher', 'teaching', 'student' and 'learning'. It also looks at the aims and problems associated with education, how teaching should happen, what should be taught, how to find the balance between providing knowledge and indoctrination and so much more. Philosophers have argued over school education for centuries.

Here's my philosophy about education and life.

There are three things over which we have control:

1. *Our vantage point*
2. *What we think*
3. *What we say.*

This is the message I'm conveying to you in this book. Your vantage point is constantly changing and your understanding of schools, schooling, education – and your role in each – is growing. The more you learn about school education, the more impact you have by what you think, ask, do and say.

Just keep reminding yourself: *'I'm moving from the unknown to the known, just like everyone else – including teachers'.*

Our aim is to use what we know and learn more to understand school education more easily, support it more effectively and help it succeed.

SCHOOL CULTURE AND BELIEFS

Schools are often guilty of using wordy statements to describe their beliefs and culture. They might sound impressive but they don't really say a lot – probably because beliefs and culture are not easy to describe.

You might find a statement of philosophy published by your children's school. Chances are, you'll also find descriptions of belief included under other headings. Examples include 'mission' and 'vision' statements, 'aims' and 'values'. Some schools publish 'key improvement statements', 'strategic priorities', 'context challenges', 'intent and rationale' or 'strategic pillars'.

Don't be alarmed if your head is buzzing and you need some clarification. A quick Google search will show you how organisations and individuals define these or other similar terms; the problem is they often mean different things or the meaning isn't clear at all.

A good starting point – and a good idea – would be to expect a 'shared language of agreement' on these terms. From, there, I recommend that schools place values, mission, vision in that order.

1. **Values:** beliefs that drive behaviour and create the culture
2. **Mission:** the schools purpose and contribution
3. **Vision:** how the school makes its values and mission visible

School documents would then be easier to write, understand, adapt and apply.

In the meantime, let's look at five statements taken directly from one primary school document that attempts to describe its vision and values.

'Nurture our student's desire to learn throughout life and foster their capacity to exercise judgement and responsibility in matters of morality, ethics and social justice.'

'Partner with our students on their life-long journey of learning and discovery – so they may participate meaningfully and with purpose in a world they are already helping to shape.'

'We learn through consciousness of thought where we re-configure pre-existing understandings and concepts.'

'Be inspired by the school vision and the demonstrated impact of our collective community to make a positive difference.'

'Children, parents and teachers are continually involved in active research, developing the evolving vision and practices of the school.'

What are your thoughts on these statements? Reread them, giving particular thought to relationships and partnerships.

You know my position. I don't believe that people who work in schools have equal responsibility for your children. For me, school education isn't a 'partnership'. Schools are part of the ever-evolving ebb and flow of people who have a relationship with, and influence on, you and your children.

I noticed several things in these statements: there is a reference to 'children' and 'students'; 'partnership' is used, rather than 'relationship'; nurturing is said to be provided; there is no mention of teaching. I have questions: Whose 'morality, ethics and social justice' is the school referring to? Is the world currently being shaped by how the school nurtures children rather than by what students are taught? What understandings is this school re-configuring? What research is being conducted and how well is it understood?

I realise there's a long list of statements and you might think my position is a little over the top. Here's a suggestion:

Look at the statements, then look at my observations and questions, if you like. Now go back to my first question: What are *your* thoughts on the school's statements?

Remember: words matter! Be careful of blind faith. Have faith in your own 'judgement'.

This is how I interpret this particular school's philosophy:

'Your children's lifelong moral and ethical judgement will come from the reconfiguring of their ideas, through the partnership they have with their school and onsite research – probably when you're not around.'

Give it some thought. If it has sparked concern and the need for debate, that's a good thing.

Let's move on to another statement. Here's one from a senior school.

Our statement of values and school philosophy ensures that everyone in our school community will be treated with fairness and respect. In turn, we will strive to create a school that is inclusive and safe, where everyone is empowered to participate and learn.

Now – and forgive me again for being critical – let's look at the first sentence. A statement doesn't ensure anything; behaviour does. As for the second sentence, if striving to create an inclusive and safe environment is a priority, what does the current teaching and learning environment look like? Is it divisive, unsafe and disempowering? There is no reference to 'teaching'; perhaps that's why!

A school's philosophy should be understood, seen and felt. That's what is meant by school culture.

What about these statements?

Our school vision is that the instruction we provide continues to help parents in the education of their children, just as it does today.

Our school mission is to teach an agreed specified curriculum that can be applied to personal goals and aspirations.

Do they respect your position as parents? I think they do.

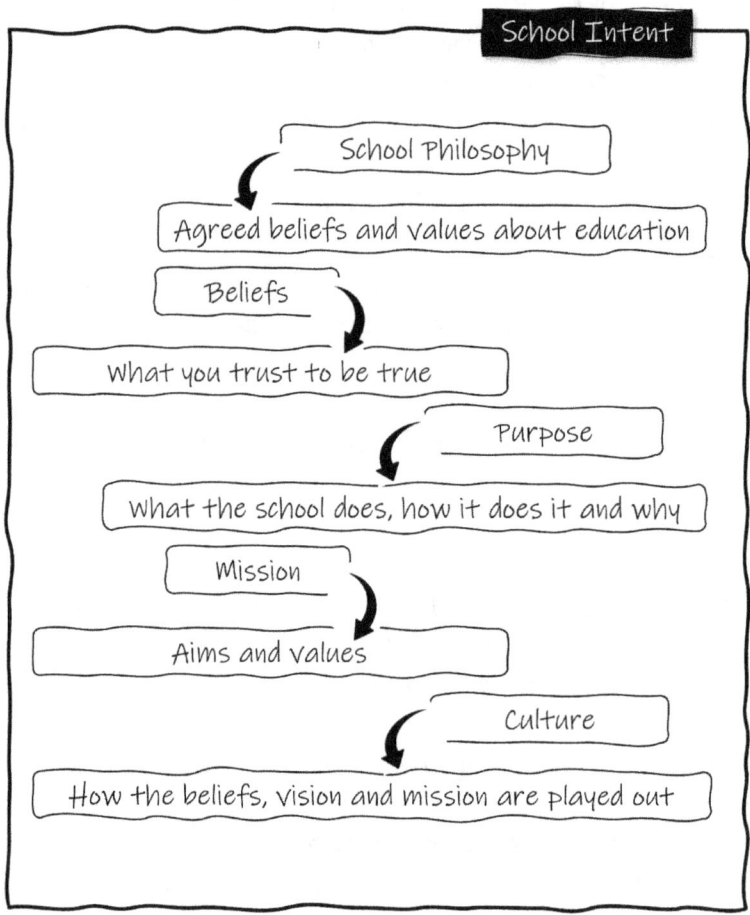

Expecting a 'shared language of agreement', particularly on statements like the ones you've just reviewed, is critical. Use this visual as a starting point for thinking about whether these descriptions resonate with you or need adapting.

And consider this; if you can't explain it, you can't apply it. The simpler school documents are, the better they are understood, applied, measured and adjusted.

A PHILOSOPHICAL POINT OF DIFFERENCE

Through a friend, you hear about a senior school that boasts 'a paperless, book free and computer only environment'. Does this describe its philosophy?

What about these?

School 1: *Be inspired. Be amazing. Be yourself.*

School 2: *Where learning comes first.*

School 3: *Learning for learning's sake.*

School 4: *Everyone is valued, respected and challenged.*

School 5: *Value. Engage. Empower. Young women for a global future.*

School 1 sounds like it could be encouraging independent thought and action. It's possible School 2 could be more interested in learning than teaching. School 3's statement really worries me. Are students encouraged to strive toward goals or do as they please? School 4's statement is confusing. Isn't that what everyone in every school should be? It doesn't tell me anything I shouldn't already know or expect. As for School 5, it's clearly a single sex school that encourages girls to become women of the world.

There's a lesson here. Schools like to market 'themselves' in creative ways. Be careful not to fall into the trap of believing what you read in blind faith; you want to see beliefs in action.

That's why it's so important to have a clear understanding of your own values and beliefs.

THE WHO'S WHO OF PHILOSOPHERS

Here's something that might interest you. For centuries, philosophers have argued about what makes a 'good society' and have asked 'why be good?' Every argument suggests education will lead to the answers.

As you would expect, views from one extreme to the other have been thought about, debated, published and followed. By learning about philosophers and their beliefs, we gain a better understanding of what makes us think and question what we do and how we do it.

Some people believe strongly in socialism or communism. Others hold the belief that capitalism is of the utmost importance. These are two extremes that influence our view of how schools operate and function. How do these beliefs address the concepts of fairness and responsibility?

The question isn't designed to prompt a political conversation but such a conversation might be sorely needed. The continuous loop of influence that socialism and capitalism have on schools, and the impact this has on families and your children's future success are topics not usually discussed.

It is well worth the effort to set aside some time to collect your thoughts and see where your view of life, education and happiness comes from. I'll get you started with the work of these philosophers. The rest is up to you. We never stop learning.

Aristotle (384BC–322BC) believed that living well is to have a strong moral compass.

Adam Smith (c.1723–1790) believed that the wealth of a community is measured by the contribution of its citizens.

Robert Owen (1771–1858) believed that education and socialism could help cure social problems.

Frances Wright (1795–1852) believed in universal education, equal rights and legal rights for married women.

Marxists, following the theories of Karl Marx (1818–1883), view schools as places that reproduce class inequality and where children are taught passive obedience to authority.

Rudolph Steiner (1861-1925) believed being human includes spirit, soul and body and that human beings develop in seven-year cycles. This underpins his view that education must include intellectual, artistic and practical skills, with a focus on imagination and creativity.

Mortimer Adler (1902–2001) believed that education is a lifelong process.

Ayn Rand (1905–1982) believed that the moral purpose of life is to be the hero of your own life, by finding your own happiness.

Do you think having a philosophy of education is important? My guess is that your answer would be yes.

Homework

WHAT'S YOUR PHILOSOPHY?

Here are 20 statements to consider, expand, challenge and discuss. Some touch on ideas we've looked at already; others cover what's still to come. Some will be easy to address; others might be challenging. Either way, they're a good starting point for you to:

- Find similarities between values you and your children's school might hold
- Discover differences between values you and your children's school might hold
- Share views with other parents and compare vantage points

Give each one some thought, be frank in your responses and don't sugar coat your reasoning. Mark up any key words you're not familiar with and which might need further exploration further.

1. My children should choose what they want to learn
2. Teachers shouldn't be expected to teach my children. I would prefer they facilitate my children's freedom to learn what they like, when they like
3. I believe in both teacher-centred and child-centred school education
4. My children must learn about worldwide problems
5. My children must be taught essential content in English and Mathematics
6. History and Geography are essential subjects
7. I expect my children to rote-learn times tables
8. Handwriting is an essential skill that I expect my children to be taught
9. My children should be in class with friends their own age, despite their academic success.
10. School uniforms are unnecessary

Thinking About Philosophy

11. Teachers should be called by their first names
12. My school should use gender neutral pronouns
13. I don't believe in report cards. I want my children to be assessed on group activities and outcomes
14. I believe in competition
15. My children must be prepared for the workforce
16. I expect teachers to share their views on issues such as climate change
17. I believe in reward and punishment
18. Every school should have the same values as those of our country
19. I disagree with tests
20. I believe every school should have the same resources as the most expensive school in the country

Thinking About Philosophy

Family Time

FAMILY AND SCHOOL PHILOSOPHY

There's no degree available for raising children. Your upbringing and life choices play a major role in the choices you make. People around you will also influence your choices, including people connected to your children's school.

You might have guessed you'd be encouraged to talk about your own philosophy on family life and the philosophy of education at your children's school.

That pretty much sums up this family time exercise.

You might like to use this short list of ideas to get started.

You might also like to ponder these questions:

1. Is your philosophy of 'family life' the same as the one you grew up with?
2. You're an influential teacher for your children. What do you teach well?
3. What are the good things you notice about your children because of how you have chosen to raise them?

---

1. Visit a book shop and browse through the philosophy section
2. If you're interested in purchasing a book, try to find one that offers an overview of a range of philosophers
3. Visit your school's website and look for philosophies and mission and vision statements
4. Go online and look at 'philosophy for children'. The language is usually much easier to follow
5. Make lists of values you have and talk about where they came from
6. Share stories about the people who have influenced you most and what they have taught you

Learning About Philosophy

APLL Group

PHILOSOPHY OVER COFFEE

What is the philosophy of the school your children attend or plan to attend?

Visit the school's website and find its philosophy, its vision statement and its mission statement.

Print them off or write them down, and then complete these 5 short tasks:

> 1. Underline any words or phrases that could have more than one meaning or interpretation
> 2. Discuss the value of the statements
> 3. Identify where there is agreement and where there are differing points of view
> 4. Document any questions left unanswered
> 5. Does the school live up to these statements?
> 6. What evidence is there that it does or doesn't?
>
> *Exploring School Philosophy*

Try to organise a way to share your thoughts with other parents and, perhaps, teachers.

Believe It or Not!

Sze Ting's school required us to attend a re-enrolment meeting. It was held online and the interviewer was a teacher Sze Ting and I had never met.

During the meeting, the teacher read out a *Student Code of Conduct Statement*, relating to onsite and online behaviour. Ting was asked to agree to the statement, which she did.

The teacher then read out a *Parent Code of Conduct Statement*. I was asked to agree to the statement, which I did.

I asked whether there was a *Principal, Teacher or Staff Code of Conduct Statement*. There wasn't one.

During our meeting, this teacher was seeing the student and parent codes of conduct statements for the very first time. It was also revealed that the teacher, and all the other teachers who were running re-enrolment meetings, had been instructed to follow an identical process.

The experience demonstrated a great deal about the value placed on different school community members. It was as though school employees were above the law.

Wrap Up

- **LESSON 1:** A school's philosophy should be easy to understand. It should respect your right to fulfil your responsibility for your children's education and your children's right to have your protection.

LESSON 2:
Pedagogy and Personalised Learning

General information you receive from your children's school is usually linked to the school's philosophy and policies. More targeted information about your children, including report cards, is very much influenced by two principles: pedagogy and personalised learning. Both of these are linked to how teaching and learning is taking place in the classroom.

You already know how important your school's philosophy about teaching and learning is. You must also be familiar with *how* your children's teachers interact with your children during the teaching and learning process.

As with most ideas about school education, there's often confusion about what is meant by terms such as 'pedagogy' and 'personalised learning'. This once again highlights the importance of a shared language of agreement. As you're reading, if you find yourself disagreeing with what I am saying, then challenge me.

PEDAGOGY

The most commonly held definition of pedagogy is 'the art and science of teaching'. In practice, that's the combination of teaching methods, learning activities and learning assessments. Basically, it's about leading children in *what* they learn and *how* they learn.

All teachers have their own unique pedagogy. I like to think of pedagogy as a teacher's DNA. It's a fascinating topic and attracts various interpretations, support and criticism.

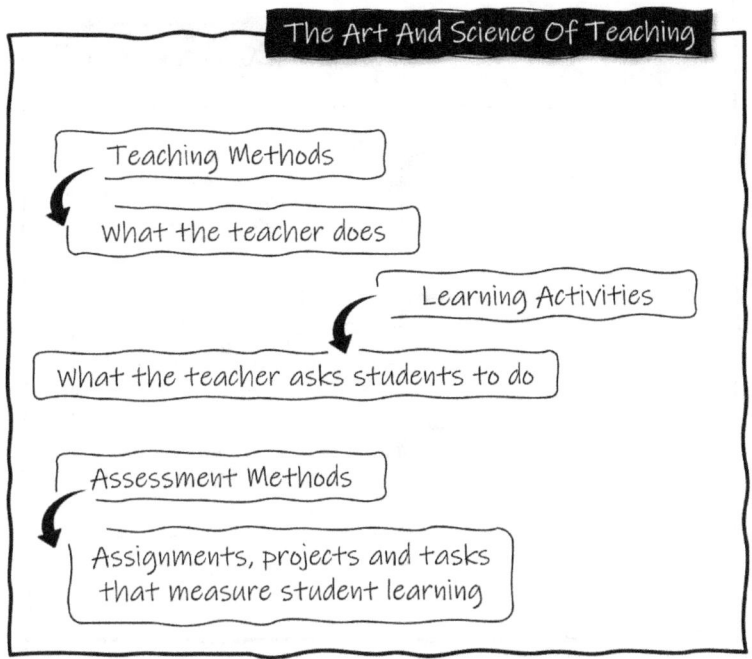

As you know, it's impossible to have teaching without learning or learning without teaching. Perhaps that's where pedagogy can get rather tricky.

Stay with me. I don't want to complicate things. There are two other terms related to teaching and learning that you might have heard. The first is 'andragogy' which is about leading adults. The other is 'heutagogy', its fundamental principle being learner agency.

In schools, *learner agency* is usually used instead of the word 'heutagogy'. In schools that use this approach, students take responsibility for their own learning and make decisions about what they will learn and how. They also measure what they have achieved. You'd be right in thinking it's a method for preparing students for lifelong learning.

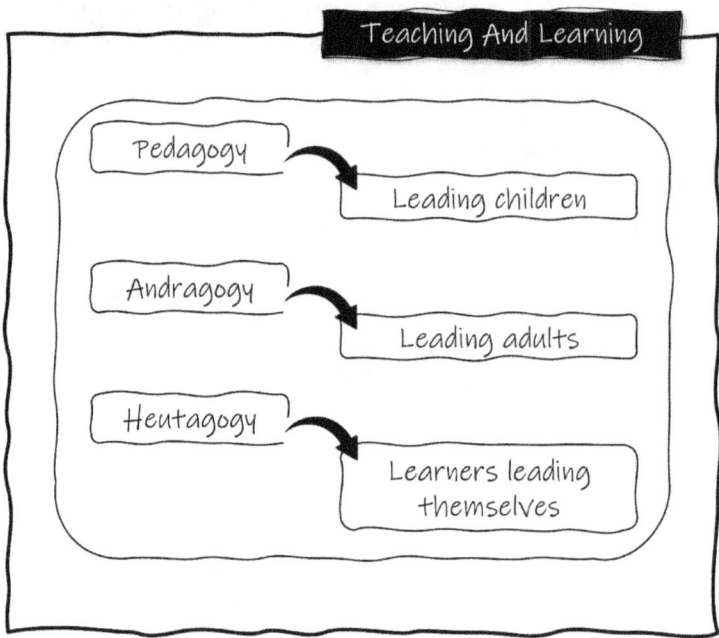

Why have I shared these terms with you?

It's because no two teachers are the same. If a school elects to give teachers the freedom to choose between pedagogy and heutagogy, then you'll need to know. Likewise, if a school believes all teachers must operate classrooms based on the principle of heutagogy but some teachers believe children require more discipline and guidance, you need to know that, too.

As a parent, you sometimes teach your children and, at other times, you encourage them to learn for themselves. There's room for both, depending on the circumstances. Perhaps the same could apply in classrooms. What do you think?

CONSCIOUS PEDAGOGY

Here are lists of other factors that influence pedagogy. I constantly adjust this chart, after discussing the factors with colleagues and challenging teachers on their approach to education.

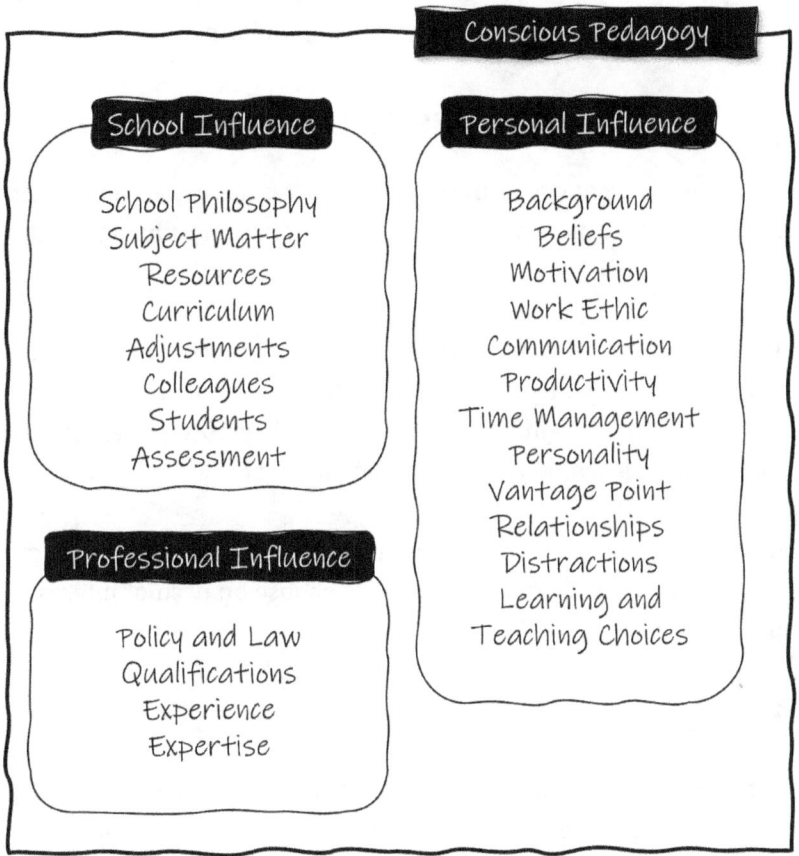

The *Conscious Pedagogy* visual is a handy resource that shows the influence just one person can have on your children's education. Multiply that by the number of teachers your children have over the course of 13 years or more.... It's well worth thinking about.

Be sure to revisit this chart as you keep learning. You'll find, just as I have, that your views and knowledge of each influencing factor will grow and change. I know you'll question some of them.

Don't be afraid to indulge in a little creative mapping. The chart isn't set in stone. Adapt it or develop your own visual tool. The more you personalise it, the more valuable it becomes.

The *Conscious Pedagogy* chart might also be useful for helping you in communication with your children's teachers. If there is clarity required, or an issue of concern, the chart can help you explore what might be the cause and where the potential solutions could be.

You could go further and consider other 'influencers' – from grandparents to sport coaches. Think about their approaches to teaching and its benefits for your children.

PERSONALISED LEARNING

In everyday life, we all have different needs and capabilities. It is also true in our learning. Many schools have taken this idea a step further and have adjusted the reliance on pedagogy by introducing 'personalised learning'.

What is personalised learning? It's an approach that aims to customise learning for individual students, based on their strengths, needs and interests. It began with the creation of individual learning plans for students with special needs; now, it might involve all students in creating their own individual learning plans. The goal of personalised learning is to boost student agency.

The value of personalised learning is to introduce it at a point where children can apply what they have been taught in core areas of study. Essentially, students choose an area of interest or an elective and 'own' their learning.

That's the good news.

The bad news is that, like most new ideas that flood schools, Personalised Learning Plans have been embraced before their value has been fully understood and potential problems have been identified and ironed out.

This is especially problematic when teachers are expected to apply new and different learning and teaching approaches, when they haven't had sufficient time or training to distinguish between them and the approaches they were already using, or make any necessary adjustments.

Teaching can be affected by time management difficulties, lack of prior knowledge, poor organisation, lack of resources and attitude. These things also affect your children's learning. If personalised learning doesn't take them into account, what could be of extraordinary benefit to your children's school education can be compromised. A great opportunity can be lost.

TEACHERS LEADING TEACHERS

When a new program is introduced into schools and expected to be rolled out and used in all classrooms, school leaders either undergo professional training, in order to understand the program, or they send someone along in their place.

The school is then responsible for preparing the rest of the staff for the program roll out; this is generally done using a 'train the trainer' approach. The learner becomes the teacher for the next learner. Despite the time and money spent, not all schools and classrooms will successfully deliver the new program as it is intended.

Here are a few reasons why:

- The information transferred from teacher to teacher will often not end up the same as it began. Every teacher will apply the information differently
- In some cases, time management difficulties might mean programs are rushed
- If teachers aren't fully aware of what the program offers or how all components are applied or measured, your children's education may be compromised, but so too will the teachers they are training
- The success of the program is measured only by a teacher's opinion of what's been learned; where no evidence is required, there's no accurate measure
- A teacher who disagrees with the program or some of the content will influence the way it is delivered
- When a school's philosophy includes a self-directed approach, it brings the process of train the trainer for teachers into question.

These are examples of how teacher education affects schools.

Learning and teaching for children is no different to learning and teaching for adults. The way different schools deliver the curriculum and the way different teachers in the same school deliver curriculum has a direct impact on your children and your family.

Homework

PERSONALISED LEARNING AND YOUR CHILD

It makes sense that teachers would want to match the way they teach with the way children learn. Personalised learning, if used effectively, can do this.

If your school uses Personalised Learning Plans, ask your child's teacher to explain, or remind you, how they work.

Make an appointment with your child's teacher. Be sure to state the reason for your request and agree on a timeframe of between 15 and 30 minutes.

Ask the teacher to bring to the meeting some samples of work that show the benefits for your child. Before the meeting, check your children's progress in essential areas of learning, including English and Maths.

That way, you're better placed to find out, from the teacher, the links between what your children *know* they need to learn and what they *choose* to learn.

When you attend the meeting:

- Take someone with you. Emotions can compromise good intentions and having a support or witness helps alleviate words or actions from being misunderstood or misreported.

- Be mindful of your position. You are representing your child, however you are also there to learn.

- Don't be afraid to ask questions.

Family Time

TOSS AND TALK

Play a game of *Toss and Talk* to learn more about what your children have learned at school and how they are learning.

As a starting point, use their homework tasks, a home reading book, a topic they are exploring or a comment they have made.

1. Cut out the die
2. Fold and tape it together
3. Take turns to *Toss and Talk*

Here's a few samplers for inspiration:

I see you might need some more help with research.

I feel a little anxious about what you have just said. How do you feel?

I think this is your best ever handwriting.

Have fun!

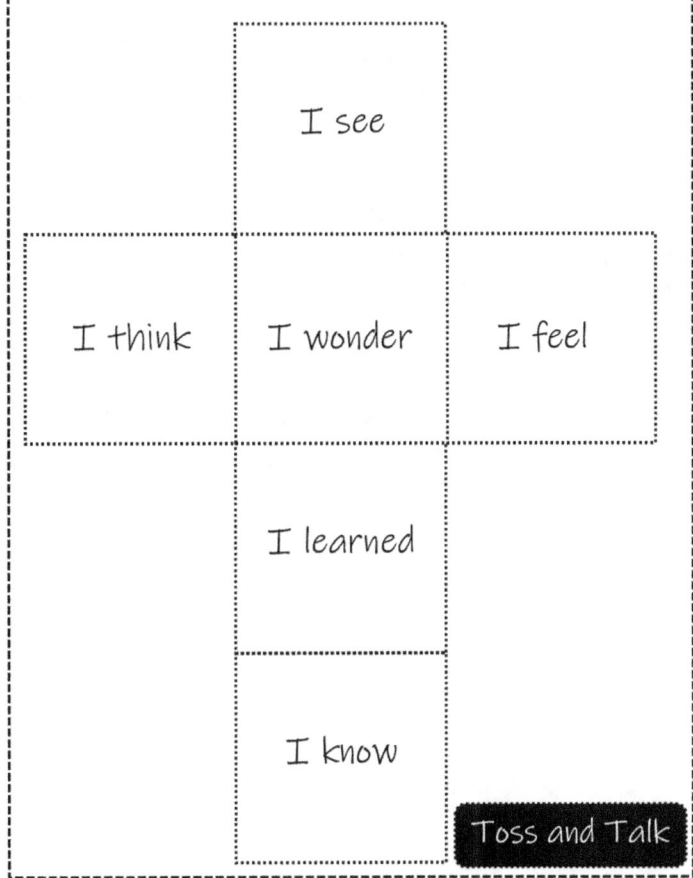

APLL Group

PARENT AND TEACHER PEDAGOGY

Since the moment your children were born, you've been their parent and teacher. You've raised them to have patience, to trust and to love. You've taught them, for example, how to ride a bike, greet people respectfully, help others and say sorry. The list goes on and on.

Then, suddenly, your children start school and you're 'just a parent'. Or are you?

Great schools recognise that you are still your children's most important teacher. Your instincts as a parent guide you and you have a special knowledge about how your children learn best and what they need to be taught.

Here are 10 principles that are relevant to your most important role as *a parent responsible for your children's education.*

Discuss, debate and decide whether these principles are part of your pedagogy as your children's teacher and parent.

> 1. Learning happens mainly through talking and interacting
> 2. Helping your children learn is an instinct
> 3. What a child needs to learn is not the same as what a child wants to learn
> 4. Real life learning makes more sense
> 5. Building on what children already know works best
> 6. Every day there is learning to be done
> 7. Sometimes planning to learn has benefits
> 8. Being flexible makes learning more natural
> 9. Learning is full of knowledge, skills, thinking and fun
> 10. Deep and shallow learning both have value
> 11. Using our hands is a great way to learn
> 12. Knowing how to use resources to learn is better than just having them.
>
> **My Pedagogy**

Peak Performance at Six

While sorting through some storage boxes, I came across some old VHS tapes. One of them included footage of a foundation class I taught in the early 90s.

Featured in the footage were two very different teaching and learning experiences.

The first clip was of the school concert. My 6-year-old students had taken a vote and decided they wanted to act out a favourite story – *Wombat Stew* by Marcia Vaughn. The performance went off like a dream. In fact, I remember everyone saying it was the best of the evening.

Knowing the students would be performing on stage in front of hundreds of people, I made sure their only focus on the night of the concert was their dancing and movement around the stage. Their lines, including those of the 6-year-old narrator, were pre-recorded. Plenty of practice beforehand and supporting each other on the night proved to be the recipe for success.

Also on the tape were interviews with each of my students. There was no acting, no preparation and no support. They went it alone and did fabulously.

Any suggestion that pedagogy has no value is false. The same applies to personalised learning and any number of other approaches to teaching and learning.

When the tools used are understood and match the desired outcome, there's nothing to do but celebrate.

Wrap Up

- **LESSON 2:** Schools and teachers can value different approaches to teaching and learning.

LESSON 3:
Those Who Teach

Teachers are just like you and me. They have strengths and limitations, values, attitudes and talents. They have good days, bad days and a life outside their work. All of these things influence their vantage point as educators.

For reasons I can only put down to generational habit, and perhaps a little guilt, most parents place an unhealthily high level of trust in teachers. For decades, thousands, if not millions, of parents have assumed that all teachers possess all the necessary knowledge, wisdom, care and integrity with regard to all children.

The truth is, they don't.

If you're guilty of putting teachers on a pedestal, take them off right now. Not because you shouldn't respect teachers but because teachers who have *earned* your respect have done so by respecting you and your children equally.

Although they might respect you and your children, I can guarantee they don't have you on a pedestal.

The teaching profession is no different from any other. Every school has its share of outstanding teachers, who take their job seriously and provide a service above and beyond expectations. And, as in any other profession, there are teachers with lesser degrees of capability or commitment.

The teacher who hands out elephant stamps and has a fabulous rapport with parents isn't necessarily more capable than the teacher who keeps to an appropriate distance, demands the best from students and isn't afraid to discipline.

A reprimand from a disciplined teacher offers a bigger lesson for your children than a collection of colourful stamps identical in number to that of every other child in the class. Your children aren't 'the best' all the time – even when they have done their best.

Your role is to identify the outstanding teachers. They're the ones who know their strengths, take action to remedy their weaknesses and eagerly consult with other experts. They're the ones who will place you at the centre of all decisions made about your children's education.

In this lesson I will challenge you. Your children's teachers are not employed to raise your children for you. What then, do you expect of their service?

GOALS AND EXPECTATIONS

You would want your children to become responsible, happy individuals who set goals and strive to achieve them. You have a part to play in this and you know that school life also has a significant role.

Think about a goal you set for yourself and how you achieved it. You take responsibility for your progress while respecting those affected by your actions. Let's say you decide to become a florist and enrol in evening classes. There's a lot to consider, including the impact on your children. They'll be disadvantaged for a short while because of your absence. In the long term, though, the example you have set pays dividends. They will see what it means to achieve a goal, take risks, make compromises or sacrifices, and be responsible for ongoing education. And they'll learn even more as you make further investments in continuing education to diversify your skills or establish your floristry business.

You would expect this role modelling to apply in schools, too. After all, the people who help educate your children were children once, with dreams of becoming a teacher. If any profession boasts a love of learning, it must be the teaching profession.

You have other expectations of teachers, too. Initially, a teaching certification requires academic study and involves placement periods in schools where theoretical learning can be implemented in a practical way. You want to be confident that there will be continuous improvements in teaching techniques, approaches to assessment, knowledge building and refinement of other skills. These are all important features of a professional school environment.

Teacher professional learning includes state-wide, school-wide, staff teams and individual options. Some is of high value to children and families; some training is tailored more to a teacher's personal goals

You would be right to expect the school to measure the value of this professional learning. High-functioning schools plan, monitor and assess this exceptionally well.

These expectations are reasonable, especially as so much money is invested in teachers' learning and development. Every year an average of $6,000 per teacher is spent on ongoing professional growth. That's serious money. And it doesn't include any of the teachers' own money they might also choose to invest.

Think about the principal at your children's school. School leaders were once graduate teachers before taking leadership roles. In the transition from teacher to school leader they would have been offered a range of professional learning options – but nothing that was compulsory. There are no required courses to become school leaders. Principals have learned 'mostly on the job' – from others who have been down the same school-to-school path.

A relatively small number of teachers set themselves the goal of becoming a principal. Some never achieve it. Many teachers have stable jobs in the same school setting for many years, perhaps decades. Others move between school communities for promotion and change.

Regardless of the goals teachers have, delivering an agreed curriculum and assessing your children's progress is what they are paid to do. In striving for other goals they must consider the impact on students, colleagues and families.

Here's another way of looking at teachers and their role – regardless of ambition. You choose your family accountant, doctor, hairdresser, dentist, church and footy team. If you're not satisfied, you choose an alternative.

In choosing your dentist, you expect them to provide a service specific to your dental health. While they have studied physiology, you wouldn't have your dentist perform knee surgery. Likewise, your family doctor or general practitioner wouldn't offer heart surgery. You would be referred to a specialist.

You rarely get to choose who teaches your children. Those who do are not experts in child development or know everything about children.

Until now, you might not have looked at schools this way. Now that you have, ask yourself whether a teacher's interests, goals and ambitions support or hinder your rightful place as #1 in your children's education? Another question: would choosing your child's teacher be of value?

If that were an option, would the process of becoming a teacher and the attitude to ongoing professional learning for teachers be viewed differently?

VALUING AND RESPECTING DIFFERENCE

In my work with thousands of teachers and school leaders, I've concluded that there are six types of teachers.

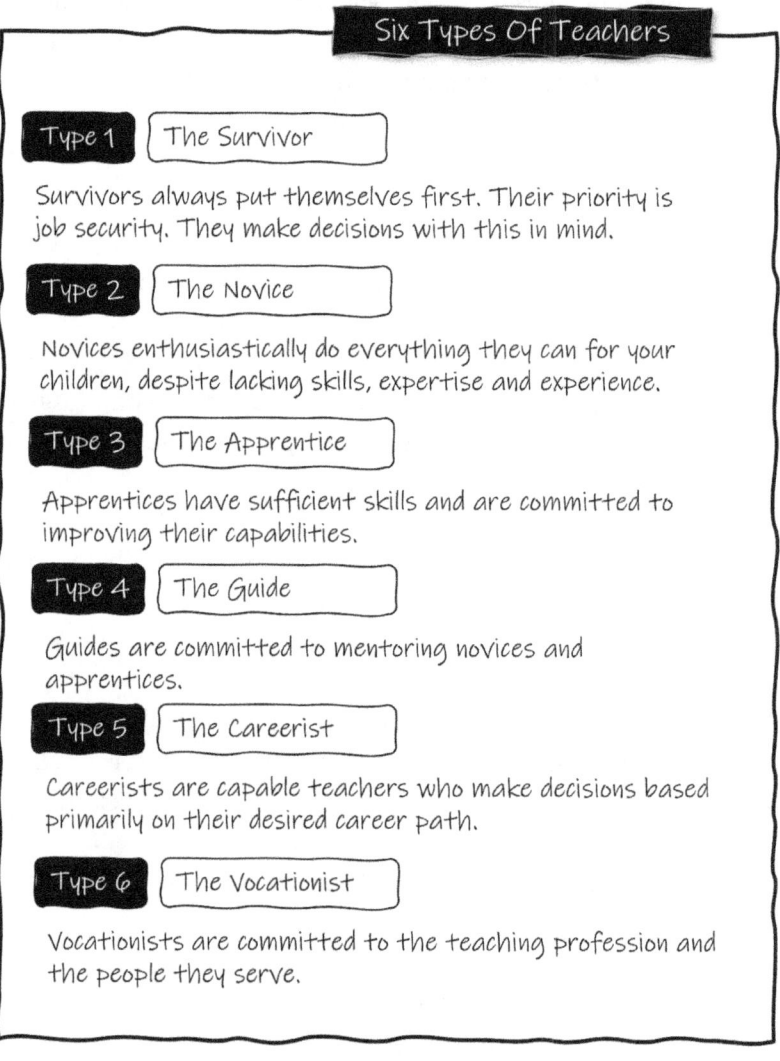

We can all share stories about the different experiences we had in schools. Many people say they don't remember what they were taught, but they remember how teachers made them feel.

I'm not too sure about that.

What I am certain of, though, is that the six teacher types just mentioned demonstrate the human side of people who have chosen to teach for a living.

It would be rare to find someone who entered teaching but didn't like children and cared for nothing more than the holidays. The way governments structure school systems and the school day isn't usually why people choose teaching as a career and certainly not a vocation.

A person's worklife has its benefits and its limitations. The key is in the word: it's about work and life. Like other workers, teachers go home after a day at school. They need boundaries to separate their work from their life and parents need to understand that teachers' priorities, outside of school, influence their vocational choices.

I have worked with all six types of teachers. I can honestly say that each one pays dividends to your children. It's not so important to seek out the most career driven teachers or focus on their personal life choices but rather to be sure your focus is on the best educational interests of your child. Have the tenacity to find out *what* is being taught and *how* teachers are educating your children.

One more thing: your children will never get *your* idea of the 'perfect teacher' every year.

CONFLICTING PRIORITIES

Whether your children attend a government, public, independent, Catholic or alternative school, their teachers will have graduated from university and will have been registered by the state in which they work.

One of my publications is titled *The Ultimate Parent Teacher Interview*. In it, I stress the importance of learning about *who* is teaching your children. It goes with your knowledge of *what* is being taught and *how* teachers are educating your children.

When a school promotes subject offerings, wouldn't you want to be guaranteed the best possible teaching as well?

Unfortunately, the best possible teaching isn't always available. Schools have long held the belief that they should offer the entire curriculum rather than match curriculum offerings with available resources, including teacher capabilities. 'Out-of-field' teaching is the result.

Out-of-field teaching happens when principals allocate a subject to teachers who have not studied the subject themselves, as part of their teacher training. It means they have limited experience and expertise in the subject.

You'll be shocked by this statement: more than 50% of teachers are involved in out-of-field teaching. A shortage of experts in certain subjects is blamed for this situation. Not widely discussed are the offers of extra teaching loads for existing staff, and the promise of job security conditional upon an 'out-of-field' subject being taught as part of a teacher's employment.

In most of these cases, schools won't say a subject can't be offered due to a lack of teacher expertise. The subject will simply be offered and, unless you inquire, you won't know the capabilities or limitations of the teacher.

The other problem area you need to be aware of is the way teacher leave is managed. Schools usually have a bank of relief teachers to cover staff absences. Teachers are certainly entitled to use their leave – that's not in question. The issue is the quality of the relief teacher.

In some schools, casual relief teachers are very highly regarded. These teachers have many years of experience and are well qualified to move between classes. In others, relief teachers take more of a supervisory role than a teaching role. Another word for it is 'babysitting'.

Your school should notify you every time a relief teacher has replaced your children's regular teacher. If this isn't happening, it needs to be addressed.

Homework

THE PARENT-TEACHER RELATIONSHIP

A parent-teacher meeting is usually limited to 10 minutes and even as few as 5 minutes in some schools. With such time constraints, how does a teacher decide what to share and what to leave out? How much time is available for a Q and A or, more importantly, for joint decision-making about your child's learning?

How can you possibly build a genuine relationship with your child's teacher?

Here's how:

Step 1: Request a meeting

Step 2: Find out what your child likes about the teacher

Step 3: Find out whether there is anything about the teacher that worries your child

Step 4: Write down any concerns you want to raise

Step 5: Read the list of possible questions provided

Step 6: Pick a few to get started.

> **Possible Questions**
> - How long have you been teaching?
> - At which other schools have you taught?
> - What was your subject major during pre-service training?
> - What do you most enjoy teaching?
> - Beyond teaching, what other school responsibilities do you have?
> - Do these responsibilities take you away from the classroom? If so, who teaches my child during that time?
> - Do you have the support you need to manage your workload?
> - How can I help you to help my child?
>
> **PT Relationships**

When I say, 'pick a few', that's exactly what I mean. This isn't an interrogation and it's not a good idea to take a list with you. If we want teachers to be treated as professionals, then we need to demonstrate it. The questions can be part of the general conversation.

Having this conversation, to learn about your children's teachers, is a positive step toward fruitful discussions in the future. It will be particularly important if you require education services for intervention or for advancement of your children's skills, talents and needs.

Remember, this is all about developing a relationship between families and schools and showing respect for one another's responsibilities. The better you understand your children's teachers, the better able you are to support them, and the school, in teaching your children well.

Family Time

THE BRIDGE BUILDING EXERCISE

It's easy to point the finger of blame at someone else and it's just as easy for someone else to point one back. That doesn't help anyone when there's a problem with the family / school relationship.

Not every teacher is the ideal one for your children and your children aren't always the ideal students for their teachers. It's a bit of a worry, though, when it happens.

What can you do?

There are so many potential lessons about building bridges for building healthy relationships.

Here are just a few important things to focus on:

- Accept differences
- Respect authority
- Speak out respectfully against unfairness
- Note the use of control and power
- Manage lack of discipline.

Have a conversation with your children about the importance of taking ownership of their learning and about your responsibility for supporting them.

Blaming others and allowing personality clashes and personal dislikes to affect you are distractions from learning. Make sure you always focus on what's best in the long term for your children.

Always be on the lookout for opportunities to build bridges that work for everyone concerned.

APLL Group

WHO'S TEACHING YOUR CHILD?

This discussion isn't a gossip session. It's a time for self-reflection and exploration of your vantage point.

Here's how it works:

1. Here are 6 types of teachers.

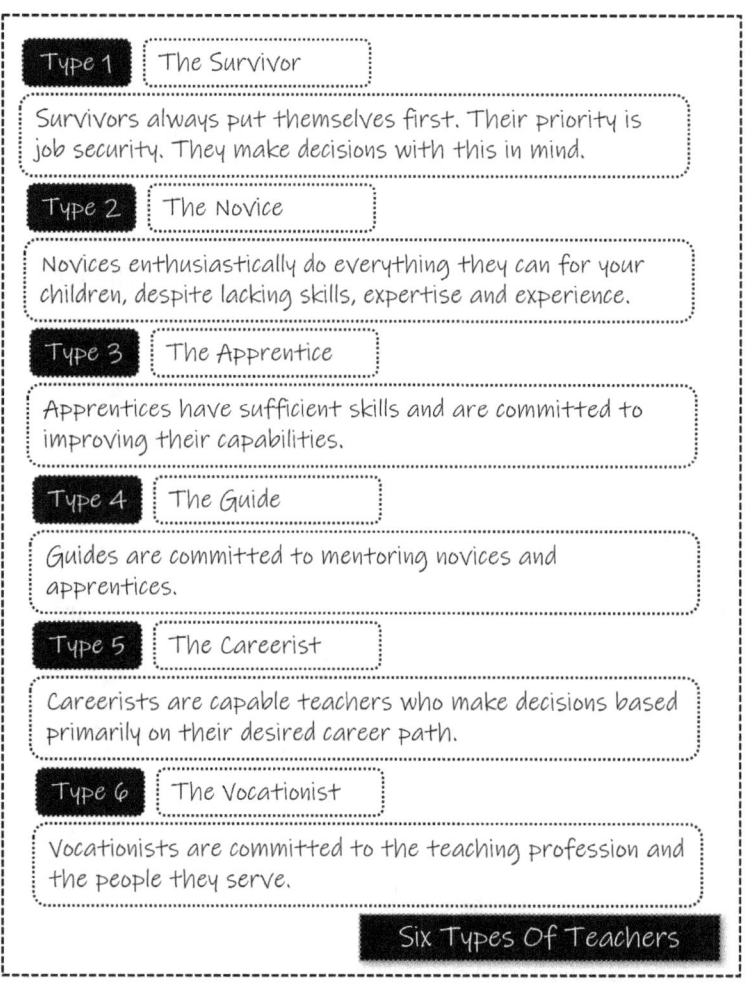

2. Read the summary of *Type 1 Teacher: The Survivor.* Talk about how the priorities of this type of teacher might affect your children. For example:

    - The advantage: Survivors do their job well and avoid internal politics
    - The disadvantage: They do only what they have to, in order to survive

3. Listen to, and challenge, each other's views

4. Might this teacher's approach provide a healthy boundary between home and school?

5. How might this teacher manage communication with parents?

Work through these steps for each of the six categories. The goal is to remove as much emotion as possible and at the same time avoid sugar coating.

You are discussing teachers, not your best buddies.

To teachers, your children are students. That's how it should be. Agreed?

Way Out of Field

Sze Ting's Year 11 History teacher was less than 10 years older than she was. The teacher had made the transition from school student to university student to schoolteacher. She hadn't studied history at university and she had never heard of Australia's most pre-eminent historian and author of more than 40 books. In spite of this, her principal gave her history classes to teach.

This didn't position her well for rich debate, critical thinking, research and comparative arguments. It compromised her teaching and the students' learning.

To make matters worse, Ting's sociology teacher was an expert in history and passionate about the subject. His history classes were offered to the graduate to fulfil a long service leave arrangement. Those classes weren't offered on his return.

I met with the principal. He held the view that all teachers could teach anything, apart from chemistry. His primary concern was protecting teacher employment.

This was out-of-field teaching in action. Teachers can, and do, accept responsibility for teaching anything asked of them, regardless of their knowledge, skills, understanding or lived experience in the subject.

It is so common for these boundaries to be crossed, there's even a philosophy to cover it: *Stay one lesson ahead of your students and you'll do just fine.*

Wrap Up

- **LESSON 3:** A university teaching degree isn't a licence to teach anything to anyone.

LESSON 4:
Curriculum Matters

Schools are places where your children gain new skills and knowledge. They learn to socialise and follow rules. They explore their own abilities and interests and, all being well, they are able to apply those abilities and interests in further learning, future workplaces and leisure activities of their choosing.

They are taught in accordance with the school curriculum.

We hear a lot about curriculum in schools and beyond. It's written about in the media. It's talked about in podcasts and on millions of YouTube videos. People have opinions about its merit and its faults. We hear what's wrong with it, that it's overcrowded and why it needs to change.

Then we have the 'culture wars' that cause conflict over values, beliefs and practices. They, too, have infiltrated our schools and shifted our thinking about the curriculum. We're asked to follow or defend and protect some values and outlaw others. This causes even more conflict until there's so much noise many switch off and the divisive curriculum lives on.

All these conflicts and difficulties with the curriculum exist. But there's an even bigger problem: there's more than one curriculum. It's time for us all to wake up.

WHAT IS CURRICULUM?

A curriculum is a course of study. Its purpose is to describe the things to be taught. A curriculum can be found in childcare settings, kindergartens, schools, colleges, universities and training programs.

You already know these are not the only places where your children are educated. They are constantly taught by others and constantly involved in self-teaching and self-learning. The sources of teaching and learning are unlimited. We all learn, change and grow throughout our lives.

That being said, you also know a school should be offering an agreed curriculum. You've read this a number of times. It's a fundamental principle of school education.

It's up to you to make sure your children are taught what they need to know so that, over time, they can pursue what they want.

Discovering the exact curriculum your children will be taught is a challenge. It is made even more difficult because Australian schools no longer teach according to an agreed specified curriculum.

A specified curriculum is an agreed non-negotiable detailed plan for explicit measurable instruction to achieve a specific educational outcome.

Schools now offer a *standard curriculum*. This standard isn't fixed; it's a moveable target. There's no fair and equal end goal for every student. Any standard your child reaches will be 'good enough', because there is no agreed specified standard to be reached.

To put it bluntly, without your input, your children risk being in educational freefall.

Let's explore this a little further.

EXPLORING YOUR SCHOOL'S CURRICULUM

Do an Internet search and you'll find websites that suggest there are 8 types of curriculum. Others claim there are 7 and others 3 or 4.

Here's a sampling of curriculum types you might come across: written; taught; supported; assessed; recommended; hidden; excluded; learned. There are also overt, integrated, core, teacher-centred, child-centred, covert, societal, subject-centred and core curriculums. Go figure!

From my vantage point, there are four you must understand.

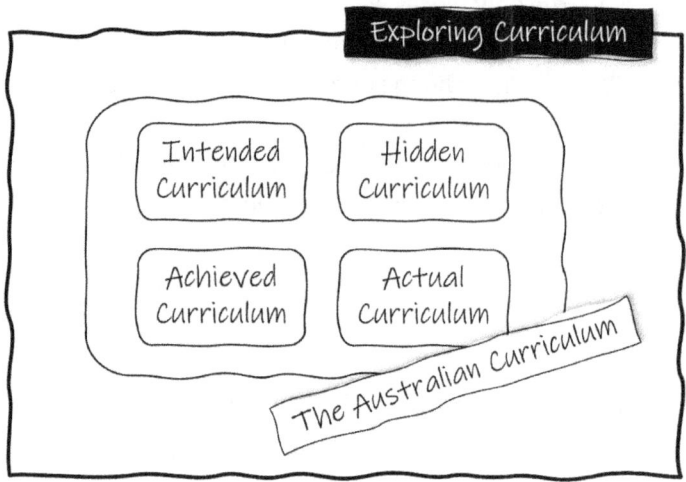

THE INTENDED CURRICULUM

The intended curriculum is the publicly available document that describes what decision makers have agreed will be taught. It usually contains written statements for each subject and for each of the year levels or stages.

The intended curriculum – in our case the Australian Curriculum – outlines what is to be taught in all schools in Australia. However, because schools in Australia are currently the responsibility of the relevant states, each state has the authority to adjust the Australian Curriculum.

And the changes don't end there. The Australian Curriculum undergoes many changes before it reaches your children. School systems, including independent and faith-based systems, also have the authority to adjust the state curriculum.

Further changes are made by individual schools.

Some schools make sure the intended curriculum has *agreed explicit measurable statements of intent* written very clearly. In other schools, the intended curriculum is tacit. These schools include statements that are vague and open to different teaching options. Some schools have a combination of the two.

Either way, the final adjustments are made by individual teachers.

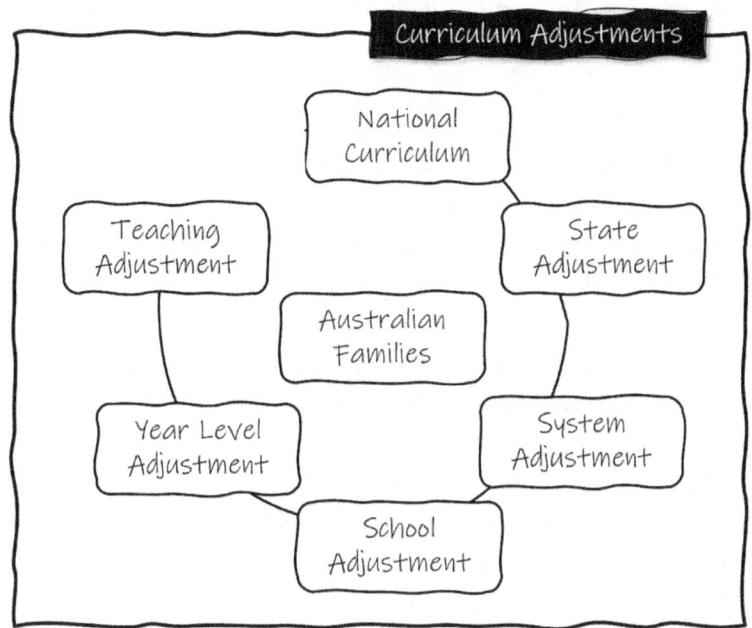

THE HIDDEN CURRICULUM

The various philosophies and pedagogies you learned about earlier lead to major changes in the curriculum, too. These changes are the result of school wide differences in perspective or of unwritten and unintended lessons that are more closely aligned with the actions of individual teachers.

Here's an example:
A Year 3 teacher begins his maths lesson on multiplication. About five minutes into the lesson, a student walks in, having just returned the day before from a family trip to Italy, to visit extended family.

The teacher welcomes the student back and politely asks her to tell the class a little about the trip. She holds up a bracelet with a charm of the Leaning Tower of Pisa and describes her experience of climbing to the top.

The teacher quickly draws a sketch of the tower and displays a map of the world. He explains Italy's location in Europe and points to Pisa.

The class is curious and hands are going up and the teacher launches into a geography lesson. The takeaway for the class is an understanding of 'their place in in the world'. The students learn that Pisa is in

Tuscany, Italy, Melbourne is in Victoria, Australia and that Italy and Australia are 2 of 197 countries in the world.

The teacher abandons his original plan and delivers what's known as 'incidental teaching' of a valuable lesson. The intended maths lesson will have to wait until the next day.

On the other hand: Imagine if the same teacher pointed to Russia on the map and spoke of the benefits of communism and his support of socialism.

In this case, the hidden curriculum is the result of the teacher's political view and is unrelated to any curriculum content or even an incidental experience that is of value.

Australia is a democratic country and is part of the 'Free World'. Australia's founding principles, guided by Judaeo-Christian values, do not support the same political beliefs as those found in communist China or Russia. Although this doesn't prevent individuals, including teachers, from holding those values, stories, anecdotes or informal comments like this, should not be shared.

THE ACTUAL CURRICULUM

The actual curriculum is fairly self-explanatory: it's what is actually taught.

Let's go back to the maths lesson. Any ideas on what the actual curriculum was in this instance?

As the teacher begins instruction on what was planned, there's an interruption and the teacher makes a switch to an unintended lesson in geography. Despite the planning that had gone into the maths lessons, the student's experience gives rise to something else.

The actual curriculum is the unplanned teaching of geography.

THE ACHIEVED CURRICULUM

If your child were in that Year 3 class, would the interruption be welcome or would it cause frustration?

Individual children learn in their own way and teachers have their own approach to planned and sometimes unintended opportunities to teach. The combined input and outcome of teaching and learning is called the achieved curriculum.

THE MISSING LINK

It's highly unlikely you can do much about these unintended situations. Until we have a movement for change that includes the reintroduction of a specified curriculum, your children's school should, however, still be able to provide clear statements of intent.

Schools that provide parents with a curriculum that outlines what their children will be taught and what they are expected to learn are taking responsibility for the current absence of a specified curriculum. It leaves no room for error or misunderstanding – and that's a good thing.

Any adjustments can then be explained. In general terms, that would mean at the state, system, school or year level. On a personal level, adjustments would mean changes that target your child's immediate needs.

If, at any time, you wish to discuss your children's learning, there are two descriptions or terms to look out for: 'explicit' and 'tacit'.

STATEMENTS FROM A CURRICULUM

Let's look at high frequency words to explore the difference between *agreed explicit measurable statements* (where there is no room for error) and *tacit* or implied achievement statements (where there is room for confusion).

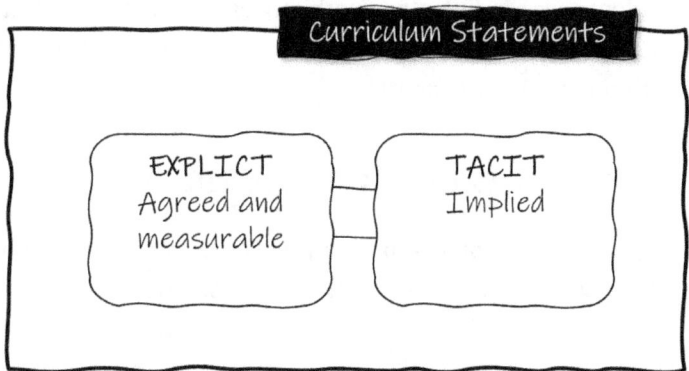

High frequency words **are** those **used** most often **in** written texts. You can see some in the previous sentence; they are marked in bold. Most schools use published lists which usually have 100 words in each. The words in each list increase in difficulty. Some schools expect children to know 100 high frequency words; others expect children to know up to 10 lists or 1000 words.

These variations don't help you much – another reason why it's important you know precisely what must be taught.

Here's a tacit achievement statement from a Year 1 spelling curriculum about high frequency words:

> *Students can read and write a large core of high frequency words.*

It states that students can read and write a number of high frequency words. It is not made clear which words or how many.

Here's a better achievement statement, also for Year 1:

> *By the end of semester one, students can read, write and accurately spell the 50 high frequency words from list A.*

There is no room for confusion here. This statement makes very clear the deadline by which children are expected to spell accurately 50 specific high frequency words.

To remove any chance of confusion there's still room for improvement.

> *By the end of semester one, students can independently read, write and accurately spell the 50 high frequency words from list A.*

Now we're clear that if students are reading along with others or copying words from the list, they have not achieved the specified expectation. This expected outcome clearly states that students must be able to spell 'independently' – that is, without support.

KEEPING UP WITH CURRICULUM

Before you start worrying about how you can possibly learn the school curriculum – especially if you have a number of children at school – there's something you should know.

You don't have control over how a curriculum is written. You do have control over what each statement means, however, and how you get evidence that your children have achieved what is expected.

My suggestion to you is this:

1. Request a copy of the school curriculum

2. Meet with your children's classroom teacher at the beginning of each term to find out precisely what will be taught and what is expected to be learned by the end of term

3. Clarify tacit statements

4. Ask for milestone meetings, where the teacher will provide you with an update on your children's progress.

You could take this one step further and arrange to have work samples for discussion before the meeting. This would give you time to chat to your children about the task, learn more about their learning and identify any challenges they faced. That way you will contribute equally to the meeting rather than passively accept the information provided.

Curriculum is designed to support your children in becoming independent and responsible citizens. Your role includes knowing what they are learning and whether it is of value – and speaking up if it's not.

Homework

A QUICK REVISION EXERCISE

It's really challenging to explain how simple school education *can* be when it has become so complicated.

You've read about all kinds of curriculum. There are many others you can still research if you're interested. Meanwhile, you can look at the visual, below. Does this help provide a picture of the key elements you have explored?

I know you're not looking for a watered-down curriculum. You expect schools to use appropriate and effective ways to teach your children so they can make choices about further study, work and leisure.

If the chart is going to be helpful in conversations with your children's teachers, don't hesitate to share it with them and refer to it during meetings with them.

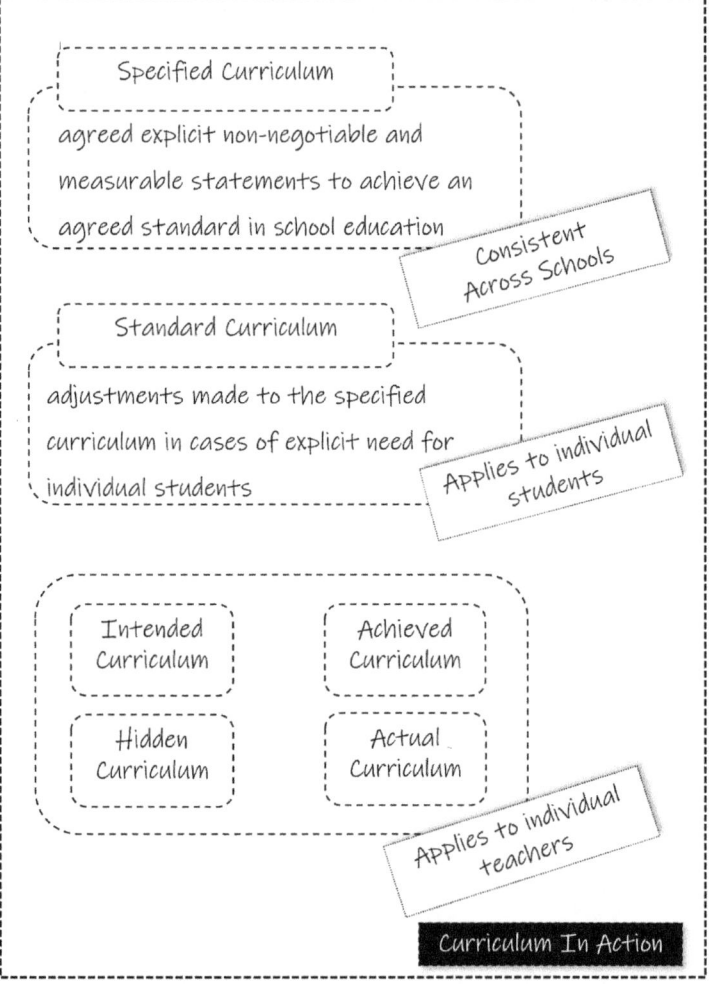

Family Time

SAME BEGINNING, DIFFERENT JOURNEY.

One of my aunts was such a talented seamstress she taught herself to design and sew wedding dresses. I can follow only basic patterns, replace buttons and sew a hem. We have diverse abilities in the area of sewing but we both needed basic skills in needlecraft.

My eldest brother became an electrician, the younger an architectural draftsman. As business owners, my younger brother and I have basic bookkeeping skills. My older brother didn't run a business. Our life choices were different but we all needed a basic education in mathematics.

Imagine where we'd be if we didn't have those fundamentals?

This is just one example of how the clear benefits of fundamental teaching and learning were so apparent in our lives. So many other pursuits – including hobbies, interests, further education and other things we wanted to do, and did – also required these foundations.

Have you heard the theory that schools *prepare children for the real world*? That isn't entirely true. What it really means is that schools should provide instruction in some of the things your children *need* when they leave school.

What do you believe those things are? Use this **Family Needs** chart to map out your family's needs and wants.

Can do	Want to do	Need

Family Needs

Earlier, you explored the concept of the whole child. This might be a good time to revisit and consider the two ideas presented. This can be especially useful if you have several children at school.

You know your children better than anyone, and every child has different interests, needs, wants and abilities.

Referring to the two whole child concepts can help you identify what you believe to be OK for schools to teach and what you believe should be guided by yourself or others.

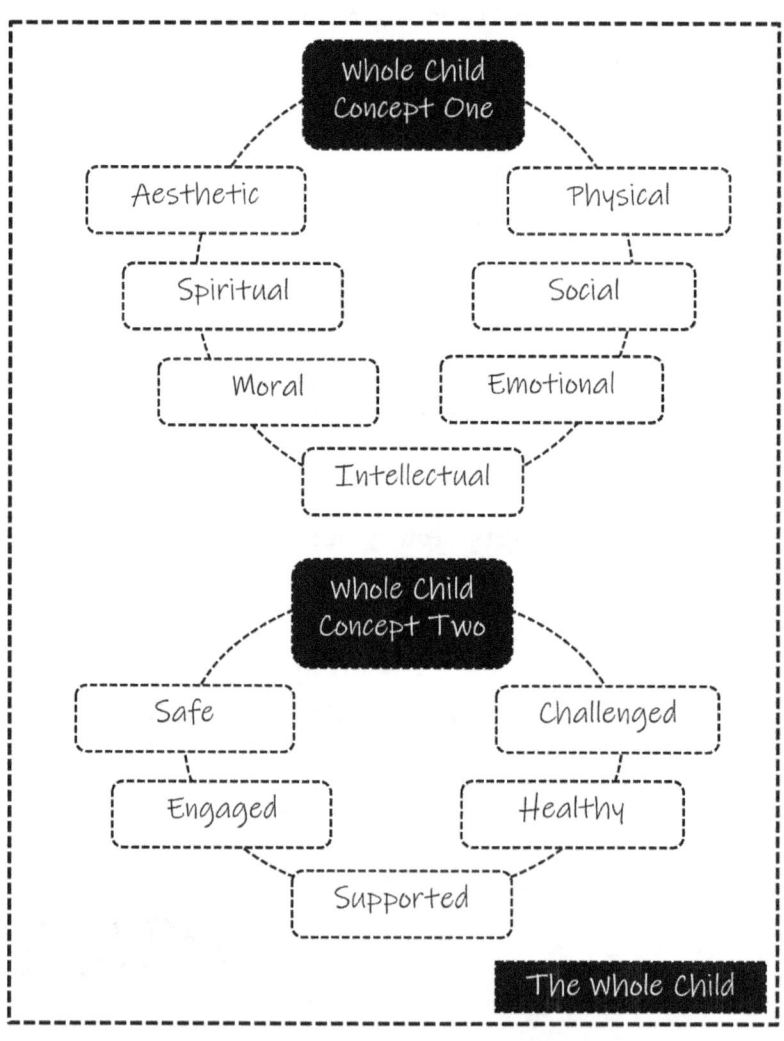

APLL Group

THINKING ABOUT WHAT'S FAIR

What do you and the other Parents Leading Learning have in common?

You might have different jobs but you all need basic skills.

You might play different sports but you all need basic skills.

There are probably other similarities you can think of.

Talk about what you *need*, before you can do what you do.

You might like to use the **Same Skill Different Application** chart to record your thinking.

Paid Work	Skill	Leisure Time	Skill	Parent Duties	Skill

Same Skill Different Application

Explain how needs are met fairly and equally today.

Explain how needs are *not* met fairly and equally today.

Use the visual below to help. If you don't like the visual – create another one.

Be sure to share your findings.

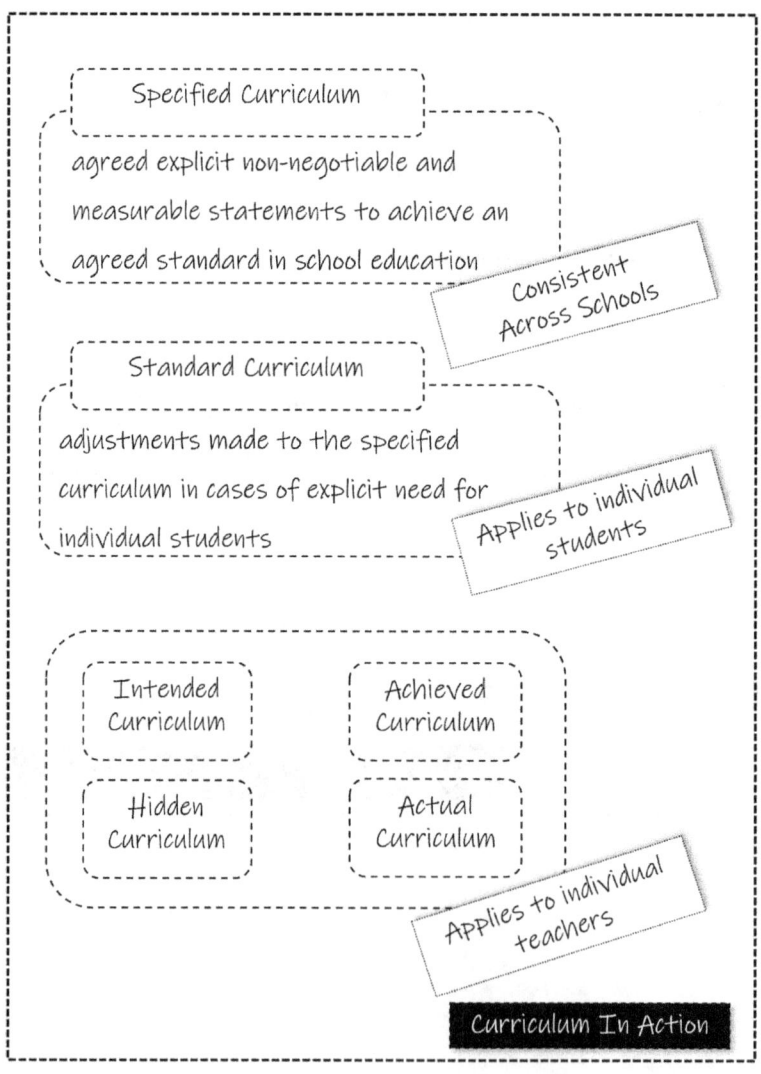

A Curriculum for Living

When Somraudee was in primary school I gave her the opportunity of a range of after-school experiences to extend her skills and interests. There were ballet classes, tennis camps, swimming lessons and competitions, piano lessons, bike education events and cooking classes. Some she enjoyed, others not so much.

During her teens, Somraudee continued her interest in piano and swimming and also developed her passion for film.

When we moved to New York, piano and swimming lessons weren't available options but her interest in film exploded. She took acting classes, had a photo shoot, purchased dozens of film scripts and became immersed in all things Hollywood and Broadway. She even met Jackie Collins and Diane Keaton.

What she learned through her interest in film couldn't be learned at school. But skills she learned at school, especially in English, helped her in her quest to learn more about film.

Wrap Up

- **LESSON 4:** There are different types of curriculum.

LESSON 5:
Reading and Beyond

What are you going to learn at school? It's probably the most common question five-year-olds are asked as they're about to begin school. The most common answer is: 'I'm going to learn to read'.

At the end of that first day, when their first *take-home book* goes into their bags, some children are thrilled to bits. These are the children who successfully memorised the book on their first day. These children see themselves as readers. They've succeeded. They can't wait for more.

For others, the first take-home book offers nothing but gobbledygook. These children experience a high level of frustration. In their eyes they have failed school on their very first day. This feeling of failure might not be obvious to parents straight away. It can fester and affect school performance in future years.

And then there are the children who don't place too much weight on their first day nor on reading. School is school. For them, learning evolves as it should and spans the good and the bad, the frustrating and the brilliant days – days they take in their stride.

The point here is that your children will begin school with expectations about learning and reading – right from day one. Your reading habits and your reflections on your own school years will also influence their expectations.

You've been there. You learned to read too.

LEARNING TO READ

Here you are reading this book. It's possible you're not entirely sure how you became a reader.

You're not alone. Researchers and educators continue to debate how children *best* learn to read.

You might receive mixed messages about how to help your children when listening to them read. You might be familiar with *sounding out the words.* This is the most common advice schools give to parents. There's no doubt it's essential. It's connected to phonics or letter-sound connections.

Reading requires an understanding of letters and sounds. *Reading well* requires other skills too.

We mustn't forget, however, that learning to read is a constant process. I'm still learning to read and so are you.

Let's see if we can make sense of reading and its place in learning English. First, we'd better agree on what we mean by reading.

The Big Reading Challenge

Here's a reading challenge for you. Seriously, it isn't too much of a challenge. Have a go.

What is reading?

Write your answer here.

```
_____

_____

_____

_____
```

Read this:

Suriyosle, it isn't too much of a chellange.

How did you go?

Even though the words *seriously* and *challenge* are spelled incorrectly you probably understood the sentence because it was predictable. You just read the same sentence a minute ago. And those words are familiar to you.

Now try this:

Aoccdrnig to rscheearch at Cmabrigde Uinerutisy, it deosn't mttaer in waht oredr the ltteers in a wrod are, the olny iprmoetnt tihng is taht the frist and lsat ltteer be in the rghit pclae.

How did you go this time?

It might have taken a little longer but chances are you managed this too.

Here's why:

1. The jumbled words aren't too long
2. Function words (to, a, be) that help join content words in sentences are in the right place
3. Unjumbling words is easier if they still sound right ('rghit' instead of 'rthig')
4. We read words as chunks, not one letter at a time
5. You already read well.

OK. Last one:

The dura mater is made up of two layers of nonelastic film. The outer layer is called the periosteum. An inner layer creates two folds for protection and security: the falx and the tentorium.

How did you go this time? If you have no idea what these three sentences are about, even though you could probably figure out each word, here's why:

1. You weren't provided with the topic or context (it's about the brain)
2. Your knowledge about the brain might be limited
3. There's a difference between figuring out what words say and understanding what they mean
4. Some of the vocabulary is unfamiliar.

Well done!

You've just succeeded in the Big Reading Challenge.

WHAT IS READING?

Let's use my simple explanation for now.

Reading is being able to figure out and understand what is written.

Notice the two distinct skills: figuring out and understanding. You might be more familiar with these terms *to decode* and *to comprehend.* These are the terms used by educators.

To decode is to convert coded messages (the 26 letters of the English alphabet) into meaningful language.

To comprehend is to understand what it all means.

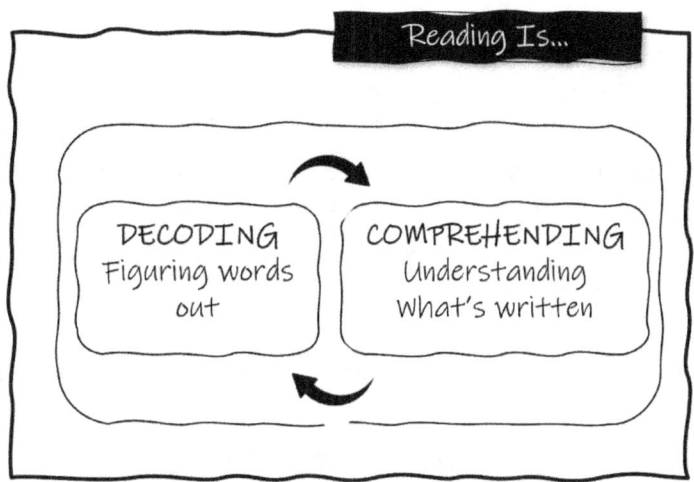

Learning to read is really fascinating. It requires you to manipulate letters to undo and construct words. It then requires you to combine words, to create greater meaning.

You've just explored this in the Big Reading Challenge.

UNDERSTANDING WHAT WE READ

It doesn't matter where you live, how much money you have, where you go on holidays or what your children do after school. Learning to figure out or decode words requires the same skills. Every school must teach children to decode effectively.

Ask your children's school to explain how they make sure this is taught.

Understanding or comprehending is a little different.

Your children have their own bank of words or vocabulary they know how to use. They constantly add to this bank through interactions and experiences, including what they do at home, what they read and what they learn at school. The more life experiences your children have, the bigger their bank of words.

Your children need every opportunity to develop a deep understanding of topics they are exploring at school.

You might not be able to change where you live or where you holiday. But the conversations you have with your children about what they are reading and learning is well within your control.

This is where you can add so much value.

You don't want them to be limited by narrow understandings or biased views.

WE READ WHAT WE WRITE

Your children will be assessed on their reading more than on any other skill or body of knowledge in school.

Reading assessments work in two ways:

1. Educators listen to your children read out loud. They listen for mistakes in decoding
2. Educators ask questions about what your children have read. They listen for understanding.

The purpose of these assessments is to find out whether your children can *read well*.

If your children spend most of their time at school reading someone else's writing and very little time mastering the skill of writing, however, there will be consequences. Learning to read is *one* part of becoming literate. It's not enough on its own.

Your children also need to be taught how to *write well*. After all, it's writing that is read. It doesn't get much simpler than that.

Learning to write text for someone else to read and understand is hard work. It requires effective teaching and practice. Time must also be spent on teaching grammar, spelling, elocution, logic and debating. Reading and writing are central to these developments.

When your children write well, they are free to express truths, opinions, feelings, ideas and more. Writing well gives your children more authority over their own lives. They're able to share their vantage point with others.

Writing well can never be underestimated. You learn a great deal about the English language when you read your own writing.

For your children to be literate, they must be able to recognise, understand, use and produce English in the right way with anyone they are interacting with. The more your children read, the better readers they will become. The same applies to their writing.

THE BIG PICTURE

I haven't explained spelling. Let's quickly revisit 'figuring out' words.

Almost every word we use has a conventional way to be written or spelled. You could say this gives all readers and writers equal access to the bank containing every word created in their language.

There are three skills used to read and write words correctly.

Phonics

Phonics is about matching *letters and sounds*. The 26 letters in the English alphabet are known by their names. They also need to be known by the more than 40 sounds they can make.

Here's an example of two sounds applied to the letter A: *ant* (short vowel), *ape* (long vowel).

Your children will need to learn all the letter-sound relationships.

Pattern

Letters can form patterns. The words *pear, pair* and *pare* all sound the same but there are three different letter patterns. You need to know the right pattern to decide which *pear, pair or pare* to use in writing. Phonics on its own isn't enough.

Meaning

We also need to know the meaning of words. Even though *pear, pair and pare* sound the same, they not only have different letter patterns, but also different meanings. We need to know what the words *pear, pair* and *pare* mean to understand what we are reading. When writing, we also need to use the correct spelling to be sure our readers know what we mean.

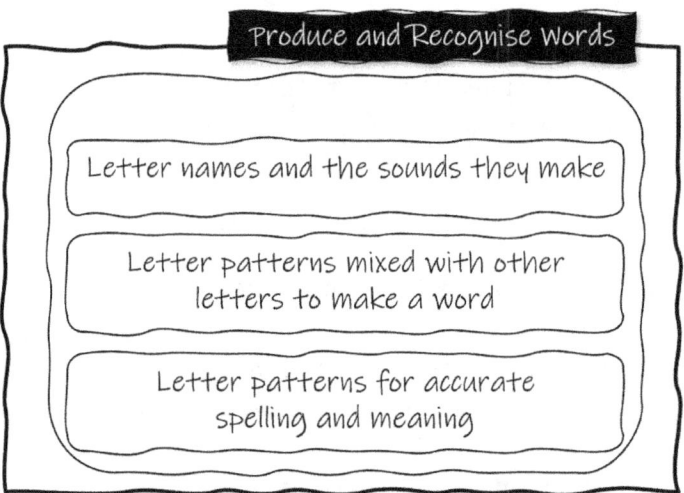

Parts of words also help with meaning. If we added *pre* (which means 'before') to the word *pare (which means 'trim', or 'make ready',* we'd have *prepare,* meaning 'to make ready beforehand'.

KEEP ASKING QUESTIONS

From the moment your children begin school, your number one responsibility is to find out what they will be taught as readers *and* writers. You'll also want to be aware of what they are reading and writing about. I can't stress this enough.

Trust me when I say you don't want to experience avoidable *parent guilt*.

I have experienced it and I've also worked with too many parents who have regretted not demanding to know more about what and how their children were learning in English classes. You don't want to learn – two, four, five or more years into your children's school life – that they are one, two or more years behind in English.

Unfortunately, this is very common.

Please don't rely on the 5-minute parent teacher interviews to get this information. Ask for regular updates on what your children are learning and whether they are at the standard they should be in English.

Take it a step further. Every term, request a *sample* of the standard of English expected of your children – in reading, writing, spelling and grammar. Only then can you intervene if they're not meeting standards.

Please understand, too, that without a good grasp of English, your children's performance in every other subject will be compromised.

MEETING ENGLISH STANDARDS

I don't know whether you're a first-time school parent or in the last phase, after a decade or more in the role. Perhaps you're somewhere in between. What I do know is that it's never too late to address your child's underperformance in English.

Your children's school should, at any time you request, provide you with information about the following:

- What is being taught
- What has been learned
- What adjustments or interventions are being made to address underperformance.

There shouldn't be any pushback against your request. You should, however, make sure you understand the procedures and the line of authority you'll need to follow when requesting information or meetings.

If there is evidence your children are not where they should be, it is more than likely for one of the following three reasons:

1. Your child needs to be more disciplined: practice leads to mastery
2. There is a problem with the teaching and learning process
3. A learning difficulty has not been identified
4. There are gaps in the intended and actual curriculum.

Underperformance can be addressed only when everyone understands what the problem is, and the role each person has in rectifying it.

You can't learn for your children, but you can be the strongest advocate for their learning.

Homework

BACK IN TIME: LESSON 1 IN ENGLISH

Here's the first of 100 *Graded Lessons in English* from a book published in New York in 1886. I couldn't resist sharing this with you. It's a master class in bringing English together.

The lesson includes reading, writing, speaking, listening, thinking and comprehending. I've adapted it for you to try out on your own. In just a few minutes you'll understand why your children must be taught to think, understand, apply and communicate effectively from day one of school.

> Back In Time
>
> Lesson 1: In English
>
> Make the sound of each letter and write it down at the same time, like this: *b – u – d*
>
> As you make the sound of each letter, form a picture of each letter in your mind: *b – u – d*
>
> Say the sounds quickly: *bud*
>
> Say the word *bud* and make a picture in your mind of what you said
>
> Write he word *bud*

This lesson, taught more than 130 years ago, is extremely powerful.

It's what becoming literate is all about.

Here's what you have learned. Be sure to share this with your children.

> An idea is represented in four ways:
> 1. The actual idea – *bud*
> 2. The picture in your mind of the idea – *bud*
> 3. The spoken word – *bud*
> 4. The written word – *bud*

Family Time

WORDS AND PICTURES

Read this word: **Dog**

Here's a word to describe the *dog*: **Big**

Here's a word to describe what the *big dog* is doing: **Barking**

Now we'll add some functional words to bring these words together. Here are two possibilities:
The barking dog is big.
The big dog is barking.

Draw or describe the **big dog barking**.

The size, breed and colour of the dog might vary, but I bet no-one's drawn or described a singing purple canary.

Read this word: Tunnels.

Now read this: **Cu Chi tunnels**

Can you picture the Cu Chi tunnels in your mind. What do you see?

Draw or describe what you see.

Your knowledge of tunnels and your knowledge of Cu Chi will influence the picture in your mind. Why not do an Internet search on Cu Chi tunnels to learn more.

APLL Group

HOME READING

Here's a quick reminder about reading.

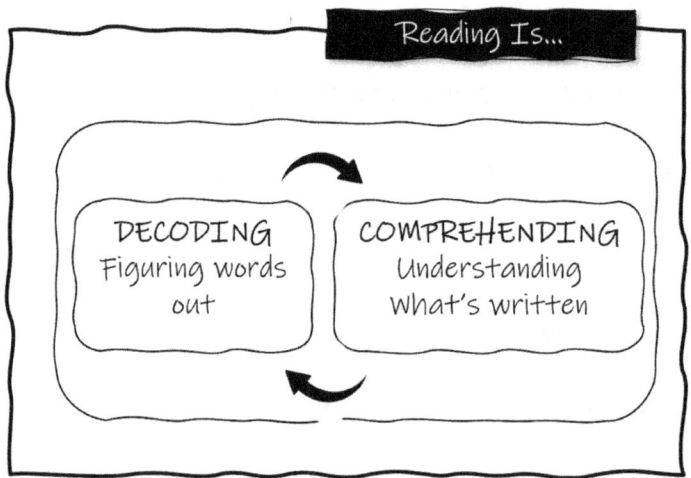

Read the following story:
Somraudee and I spent our first 12 months as a family doing the same things most families do when the children are young. Cooking, gardening, craft, dress ups, bedtime stories, adventure walks and music filled our days. Everything we did was about developing a trusting relationship, building Somraudee's vocabulary and helping her become confident in English. We were also fortunate to have a library full of children's books I'd been collecting for years.

It paid off. Somraudee thrived. When she began school, she could read simple texts and was a great storyteller. Books were a huge part of her life.

Her school introduced a new home reading program. Every day, all children were expected to take home one book at their reading level and one book of interest, plus a library book every week. The books were tattered and uninviting.

Somraudee didn't enjoy bringing them home. She wanted to read her favourite books from her home collection. We agreed she would read her levelled reading book and not worry about the other two.

Here's a conversation starter for you:
Should every child be expected to take home the same types of books or should the school personalise home reading programs? What is expected of you? What are the benefits of levelled reading books?

Things to consider:
Does the combination of schoolbooks and those available at home add to your children's reading interests?

How do you allocate of time for home reading? Is it workable for you and your children? Can you commit to a routine? Are adjustments required to maintain a healthy routine?

Have you considered a borrowing system between family and friends? It will add to the variety of books available for reading and help the family budget at the same time.

Away with the Fairies

I grew up a middle child. My brother, John, was two years older than me; our younger brother, Craig, was born in the middle of my first year of school.

Mum and Dad worked full time. Before we started school, John and I spent a lot of time with our grandparents. We learned simple mathematics by playing cards. We created imaginary worlds and went on adventures in and around the veggie garden and in Gramps' tool shed and Nan's kitchen. We made the most of simple household items, using brooms for horses and towels for capes. We climbed a ladder to get over the fence and visit Aunt Bertha, the old lady next door.

When John began school in the late 60s, I couldn't wait for him to come home each day. His first take home book was *John and Betty*. In the northern hemisphere, American children had a similar book – *Dick and Jane* – and the English had *Janet and John*.

I'd sit and watch him read *John and Betty* every day. I watched every turn of the page, his every attempt to sound out each word and every exclamation when he knew he'd made an error. I couldn't get my hands on that book fast enough. I loved the pictures and the characters. I loved being able to read it over and over again. And I loved mimicking my brother.

As much as I loved *John and Betty*, more than anything else I loved the influence my dad had on my education.

My father did two things brilliantly. The first was the way he brought words to life through his *reading*. I remember a brochure from the National Australia Bank, which was designed to teach children about saving. It included a story about the Good Fairy who saved it and the Bad Fairy who spent it. Night after night Dad read it aloud to my brother and me. His voice and intonation held me captivated.

The second was his *storytelling*. There were no brochures, no books, and no pictures – just his voice, his facial expressions and his body language. His stories had humour and humility, bravery and sacrifice, loyalty and forgiveness; they were filled with truths – and some embellishments.

Wrap Up

- **LESSON 5:** Being literate means being able to produce, understand and use English to interact in the right way with anyone.

LESSON 6:
Getting Down to Basics

You've just explored the English language. You know that our understanding of words and phrases pretty much determines the value of every interaction. It's fascinating to think that your knowledge of symbols and patterns and the meaning of words have been central to every decision you have ever made – whether in study, work and hobbies or relationships, health and family matters. The same applies to your children.

You might be blessed with the ability to speak and understand several languages. English, though, is fundamental to everything that children learn in our schools.

You also know English is not the only subject taught.

What else is on offer in schools? How have some areas of study and application become part of the school curriculum?

Let me briefly take you back to the beginnings of school education in Australia.

The passing of Victoria's Education Act in Parliament on 17 December 1872 was reported in *The Argus*, a daily morning newspaper that was published for more than 100 years. Here's a snippet of what it said:

'For the first time in this colony, the young will now have an opportunity of acquiring the rudiments of education unmixed with the leaven of sectarianism, and every child, no matter what its parents' circumstances may be, will receive at the hands of the state that key which, rightly used, unlocks whole stores of knowledge, from whose ample treasures the patient and industrious may freely help themselves.

LESSON 6: GETTING DOWN TO BASICS

'If due effect be given to the compulsory clauses, none will grow up in that gross ignorance which is such a fruitful mother of crime, which fills our gaols, and yearly robs honest industry of a large portion of its reward.

'Of course, a great deal will depend on the manner in which the new act is worked; but if care be taken to administer it in the spirit which actuated its framers, we confidently expect to see the most beneficial effects flow from its operation.'

This was only three generations ago. That's very close to home, don't you agree?

GOING BACK TO MOVE FORWARD

If I asked you to put that history lesson into one sentence, what would you say?

Here's what I'd say.
The purpose of my children attending school is to learn basic skills and knowledge that they can build on to live a free and responsible life away from crime.

Does that sound familiar?

Think about that. Just a little more than 150 years ago, people from one colony, far from Europe and the United States, had a vision that *every child could* live a healthy, wealthy and happy life. It takes your breath away.

What's even more profound is that their vision came from understanding the lives their parents and grandparents had lived. The people who established public education were children of farmers, convicts, gold diggers, explorers and marines. They had experienced wealth, crime, hope and adventure. They came together, listened to one another, agreed on what was possible and made it happen.

RUDIMENTS – FROM BASICS TO BRILLIANCE

Read quickly through this list:

- There are three primary colours but our eyes can distinguish about 10 million colours.
- To date events, some people use BC and AD (years before and after the life of Jesus Christ); others use BCE and CE, meaning (Before) Common, or Current, Era

- About 1.4 billion computer devices use Microsoft products at any one time

- European settlers brought traditional churches to Australia

- There are 12 notes in western music

- Christian beliefs were held by 97% of the Australian population in 1901

- There are 17 different sports that use a ball

- Islam was established in about 610AD

- In 1896, South Australia was the first colony where women, including aboriginal women could legally vote

- Catholic religion was established in about 30AD.

- Australians love sport; there are more than 70,000 registered not for profit sporting clubs in the country.

How would you describe the list? Fun facts, irrelevant today, a great lesson in innovation and thought or something else? What did you learn from the list and what would you share with your children?

I guess you're wondering why I've shared this list with you and why I'm curious about your thoughts. In fact, some of these points influenced the choice of subjects that would be offered in Victoria's first public schools.

The point I'm making is one you've already read. School *didn't* prepare you for everything, and going to school didn't teach you everything. It wasn't meant to. The same is true for your children.

Apart from English, then, what are some other basic subject areas to consider?

MATHS SKILLS

Basic maths skills begin in the same way English skills do – with symbols.

To learn English, your children use 26 symbols (the alphabet) and other symbols, including punctuation marks, such as full stops, commas and question marks etc.

To learn Maths they use 10 symbols (the numbers 0 to 9) and other mathematic symbols, including those for addition, subtraction and percentages etc.

Math skills are important in your children's everyday life just as they are in yours. Working with money, managing time and calculating amounts and distances, among others, are activities that require the use of mathematical concepts.

For example, knowing what should be in your pay packet, how much change to expect after a transaction and even where your footy team is on the ladder, if they win or lose, all require basic math skills. Not to mention engineering, architecture, chemistry, interior design, medicine and accounting. To do anything involving maths, your children will need to know how to add, subtract, multiply and divide basic numbers. That's just the beginning.

How much more should be taught in school?

MOVEMENT AND GYMNASTICS

Gymnastics is recognised as being the basic element in all sports. It helps develop fundamental movement skills, muscle strength and endurance, balance and co-ordination. In fact, all our everyday movements require us to use general core strength, which begins with the fundamentals learned in gymnastics.

MUSIC

I studied music as an elective for one year at Teachers College. This meant, of course, I wasn't the slightest bit prepared to teach it well enough to bring out the best in my students. I often wonder to what extent my students accepted my poor contribution to their musical education. It was clear when I was teaching music, even to my foundation classes, that I was teaching out-of-field.

Here's a little of what I should have learned, known, understood and taught.

Music is a means of communication through the creation of patterns of sounds. To read music, or write it for others to follow, we require symbols to represent those sounds. Some of the basic elements we hear in music are melody, harmony and rhythm. Music, like English, is classified into different genres and various instruments, including the human voice, produce different sounds. Music has a magical language of its own.

HISTORY AND GEOGRAPHY

If you were asked to draw a line in the sand, put your past behind you and pretend it never happened, at what age would you say you and your life became irrelevant?

That's a little harsh isn't it? But that's exactly what we're doing when we ignore history and think that it doesn't matter. Your life matters – every part of it. The way you vote and socialise, your financial success and challenges, your health, your religious views, your respect for the law and your desire to learn all form part of your life history. And all of these aspects of your life have a profound impact on your children.

That's history.

It's the study of change over time. Thinking about problems in the past and how they grew or were solved leads to the identification of patterns. If we ignore the past, we can't see those patterns – neither the negative ones to avoid nor the good ones to encourage.

People often say that Geography and History go hand in hand. I like that idea. Understanding the location of countries has helped me to understand historical events that are important to me.

One example is appreciating the distance between Ireland and Tasmania and learning about the type of ship that might have carried my great, great, grandparents when they migrated to Australia.

Another is the location of Malta, relative to the rest of Europe and Asia. On a recent trip, by visiting Malta, I was able to further my understanding of the historical events that led to the founding St John's Ambulance and hospitals.

What are your thoughts?

You could identify other obvious 'pairings', such as music and movement, sport and science or Shakespeare and English. What haven't I covered in this lesson that you think is critical for your children to learn at school? What could be learned through other life choices?

What's on the school menu of learning and teaching is a challenge and so much hangs in the balance when conflict over curriculum and subject mandates isn't resolved.

It's not easy to identify what we think should be standard for all schools and what shouldn't. It doesn't make taking the lead for your children easy for you, does it?

NO BIG DEAL. IT'S ONLY SPORT

Here's a comparison of two schools located in same community and less than 2 kms apart. You could say they are the same but different.

Let's start with Physical Education (PE), including ball skills. It's on offer in both schools.

School 1

- School 1 has raised thousands of dollars for a state-of-the-art basketball court and football oval
- The PE teacher has a degree in Physical Education and Sports Science
- Students have 3 hours of PE per week. The school offers Art and library classes as electives
- Students participate in basketball tournaments for extra development and application of the ball skills taught.

School 2

- School 2 doesn't raise a lot of money. When there is a fundraiser, any money raised is invested evenly across all areas of the curriculum, including PE, Art and library classes
- The PE teacher studied PE as an elective for one year only
- Students have 1 hour of PE per week and they have 2 hours of library per week
- There is no time for basketball tournaments.

Another interesting difference between School 1 and School 2 is that most children who attend School 1 are huge fans of the National Basketball Association (NBA). The students at School 2 aren't.

Can you guess why?

The PE teacher at School 1 incorporates into his teaching his passion for the NBA. This rubs off on the students. The teacher at School 2 doesn't do that; School 2 also has an anti-competition philosophy.

Whether your children went to School 1 or School 2, they'd be taught the PE curriculum, including ball skills, but the level of sophistication wouldn't be the same. The same would apply to Art and the library classes.

Whether the school communities or the principals made these decisions, and why, is not clear at this time. It is clear, though, that the children in School 1 and 2 do not have fair and equal access to PE, Art and library classes. Is this a problem? What about any differences there might be in Maths or English?

Should every area of the curriculum be equally available in every school?

TWO SCHOOLS - TWO APPROACHES

School 1 and School 2 are led by principals who have very different views on discipline.

The principal of School 1 has high standards of discipline for both staff and students. She invests heavily in staff professional development, holds staff and students to account for their responsibilities and expects a blend of cooperation and collaboration, depending on the tasks at hand. Classes are rarely interrupted and 95% of the lessons planned by teachers at School 1 are taught as intended. There is a high level of trust among staff and the community.

The discipline is part of the bigger picture. Not only are there three hours of PE for all students, but the principal also firmly believes that gymnastics is fundamental to all sports. A Perceptual Motor Program (PMP) operates twice a day, five days a week. Its purpose is to help younger students improve their eye-hand and eye-foot coordination, fitness, balance, locomotion and eye-tracking skills. The sessions are held on the state-of-the-art basketball court.

Older students participate in a Cadet Program, run by the Commonwealth Defence Force. They participate in fitness sessions and learn team building, survival and communication skills. This is one of more than a dozen after-school-hours offerings.

At School 2, the principal sees education through a different philosophical lens. His approach to discipline is more fluid and he is generally undisciplined himself. The students call teachers by their first names, there are no school uniforms and the bare minimum of assessment is done. There are constant disruptions throughout the school day, with unnecessary announcements broadcast over the PA system. This creates a stop-start atmosphere for teachers and students. Just 40% of the classes planned by teachers at School 2 are taught as intended and staff professional development meets the bare minimum requirement.

There is no PMP and no Cadet Program. The only after-school-hours offering is a program for children of working parents.

Which school would you choose for your child?

Homework

WHAT'S ON OFFER?

Take some time to look at the Australian Curriculum online.

Here are a few ways you can go about it.

1. Search by curriculum area

2. Search by year level

3. Do a general search to see what comes up for a specific word or phrase.

Think about what matters to you, in terms of your children's school education.

Now, thinking about what you have learned about the Australian Curriculum, compare it with the information your children's school provides and then compare it with some of your children's work samples.

Whatever you notice, it will be fascinating.

Trust me.

Family Time

LOOKING AT THE BASICS

Pick a day to 'explore the basics'.

The idea is that, for a few hours, everyone in your family will list everything they do. Things on the list could include shopping, doing homework, filling the car with fuel, turning on the oven or watching TV.

The basics for 'filling the car with fuel', for example, would be: reading the meter; understanding the cost of fuel; knowing how much you have paid; and, if you used cash, how much change to expect.

Share the lists and talk about the basics that you needed to complete each task or activity.

It's a real eye opener and a great talking point.

What else will come from this experience is anyone's guess.

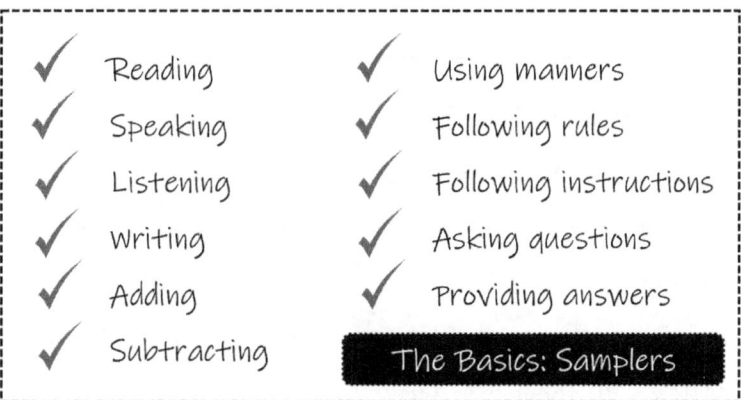

APLL Group

THE PUZZLE EXERCISE

Among the members of your group, some will have similar views; others might have widely varying ones.

What does this mean for the group's views on 'the basics' that need to be learned at school?

For this time together, you'll need post-it notes. Use them as pieces of a puzzle.

Your task is to create a puzzle that gives an overall picture of what you believe must be taught at school.

Think about the basic physical, academic, personal attributes and skills needed. You might like to add 'discipline' to the picture.

Have a conversation about this. What are your expectations of the school and your children, if good teaching and learning are to take place?

Here are a few ways you can go about it.

> 1. You can go it alone
> 2. Make it a group exercise
> 3. Go it alone, compare with others, discuss and agree on changes
> 4. If you're a parent and a teacher, it might be a valuable PD for you and your colleagues.
>
> *A Puzzling Experience*

Coming to an agreement is the challenge here. What might you do to reach consensus?

One Day You're Grown Up

Dad's father was an ANZAC. Like many men and women who sacrificed their innocence for our freedom, he was a war hero. For Dad, childhood was about surviving the impact war had on his family. It was a time he rarely spoke about directly but we learned a lot through his storytelling.

My favourite was the story of how he got the scar on his forehead. Some nights, it involved the Air Force. Other nights, it would be a tale of a spear and a local aboriginal. At other times, he told of how he was scarred as he jumped out of a wattle tree to get away from giant tree snakes. Whatever the story, he always came out the hero and we'd always fall asleep feeling safe and secure.

From an early age, without saying it in so many words, we always knew Dad had our backs. And now I'm older, I realise the hero stories reflected a longing he had for the same security – a longing that wasn't fulfilled.

To this day I have no idea how Dad really got his scar. I have a very clear understanding, though, of how I learned about the power of words and the use of the mind's eye, about the value of storytelling and about the lasting impact of learning at home.

My father was brilliant in every sense of the word. He was compassionate, wise and ambitious. He wanted the best for me and my brothers. His stories were full of honesty about life's challenges, wrapped up in age-appropriate tales and lessons that protected our innocence and stimulated our resilience. Through the gift of story, Dad gave us all he could of his own less-than-ideal childhood, including lessons about respect for history and for those who came before us.

There's a lesson here for you, too. One day you're grown up – but you're always a child.

Your childhood stays with you forever. Although you can't change it, you can be honest about what it taught you and what you have become as a result. There is much to be learned by sharing the stories and lessons of your childhood.

Be sure to share them with your children.

As you do, you'll come to realise that wanting more for your children than you had as a child doesn't require money; your childhood is history and what history teaches us is worth more so much more.

Wrap Up

- **LESSON 6:** A non-negotiable specified curriculum can sit alongside negotiable electives and other education services.

LESSON 7:
Measure That!

Having come this far in the book, you have no doubt formed many opinions and shared your point of view a number of times about what you have read. In some instances, you might have considered the importance of my stories, the quality of information provided or perhaps the value of the visual representations.

Whenever you do these things, you make a judgement or assessment of the content and, I dare say, of me, the writer.

This is what happens in classrooms every day. Teachers make judgements and assessments based on your children's behaviours and actions. They consider what your children are learning and still practising or what they have achieved in the intended curriculum. They'll notice the way your children have applied knowledge to other interests and how they reframe or alter what they've learned in new or different situations. They also make final conclusions about each student's learning.

Teacher judgements and assessment are necessary and constant components of teaching and learning.

First, a brief explanation:
Teachers make *judgements* when they form opinions and make decisions after careful thought. Judgements are often used to make 'on the spot' decisions – sometimes, but not always, about an immediate teaching moment that benefits your children.

Teachers *assess* when they collect, review and use information about your children to improve their learning. Assessment comes in many forms and occurs at different times. Not everything is assessed.

Now let's go a little deeper.

THE WHAT AND HOW OF ASSESSMENT

Background knowledge about assessment will equip you to have valuable discussions about your children's progress. You're not setting out to be an expert. Your aim is to know *what* is happening with your children's learning and *how* you can support them.

In fact, *what* and *how* questions are really useful when having conversations with your children and their teachers.

Here's an example of a question you might ask a teacher:
What was the purpose of the assessment and *how* did you assess my child?

Here's a possible response:
My aim was to ensure your child had understood Chapter 7 before moving on to Chapter 8. It was a formative assessment, made using our standard rubric.

Let's examine this response. You learned that your child needed to understand part of the book being read before moving on. You also learned that a rubric was being used.

To avoid making things any more complicated than they have to be, we'll find out several things: what teachers are looking for; the three main assessment types they use; and a list showing how teachers might go about making assessments, with a few examples.

WHAT TEACHERS ARE LOOKING FOR

I'll use a familiar shopping scenario to describe what teachers are looking for.

You're at the delicatessen about to buy some ham. The shopper in front of you requests 250 grams of honey ham. You're impressed that he knows exactly how much to order and you wonder whether his choice was based on the cost per kilo or on how much was actually needed.

You're up next and you ask for 'just a handful' of honey ham.

Two different shoppers – same outcome. The honey ham is weighed and payment is based on the cost per kilo. You could say, despite the different ways the ham was ordered, it came down to an exact science. The quantity of the honey ham determined the price each person paid.

In school, this exact science is called a *quantitative assessment*.

A spelling test is a good example.

Let's say your child gets 19 out of 20 on a spelling test. Your child has spelled *should* as *shoud*. There's no half-point for getting the word almost correct. Spelling is either accurate or it's not. There's no score for an error. The score your child received is an accurate measure of accuracy in spelling. Mathematics is another common discipline where quantitative assessments are used. Accuracy is a valuable way to measure your children's learning because there is usually no room for error in the final assessment result.

Back to the deli just for a minute. Honey ham is one of many types available, each with a different price per kilo – a cost based on the quality of the ham.

Square ham might be the cheapest; maple ham might be the most expensive. The store has made a judgement that maple ham is of the best quality. Your assessment is that honey ham is the best. The assessment you and the store have made is based not on price but on taste or opinion.

Teachers gather information about your children that can't easily be measured or translated into numbers. Neatness of handwriting, an oral presentation, a piece of artwork and a poster are some examples.

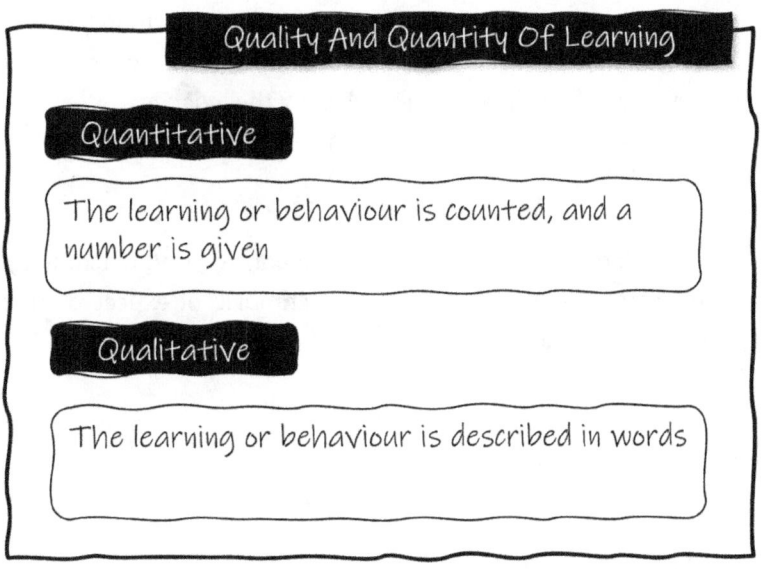

The main difference between quantitative and qualitative assessments is that with a qualitative assessment, it doesn't matter who makes the assessment. The same value of accuracy will be recorded.

Qualitative assessment, on the other hand, might vary, depending on the point of view or opinion of the person making the assessment.

To sum up: Teachers are looking for the quality and quantity of your children's learning.

THREE MAIN TYPES OF ASSESSMENT

Teachers use three main types of assessment: diagnostic, formative and summative.

Diagnostic Assessment

When you think 'diagnostic' think 'diagnosis'. A diagnostic assessment is used to identity strengths and weaknesses. In schools diagnostic assessments offer a snapshot of your children's capabilities and needs, before learning and teaching begin. These assessments can apply to you too. A parent survey or questionnaire is a good example.

Formative Assessment

Formative assessments are done to determine whether teaching or learning needs to be modified along the way to achieving the desired end result. An example that immediately comes to mind is a discussion, or a question – either intended or incidental – asked by the teacher.

Summative Assessment

A summative assessment is what happens at the end of a learning and teaching cycle. Evaluations or judgements are made and compared with particular benchmarks or expected outcomes. Exams, book reports and spelling tests are some examples.

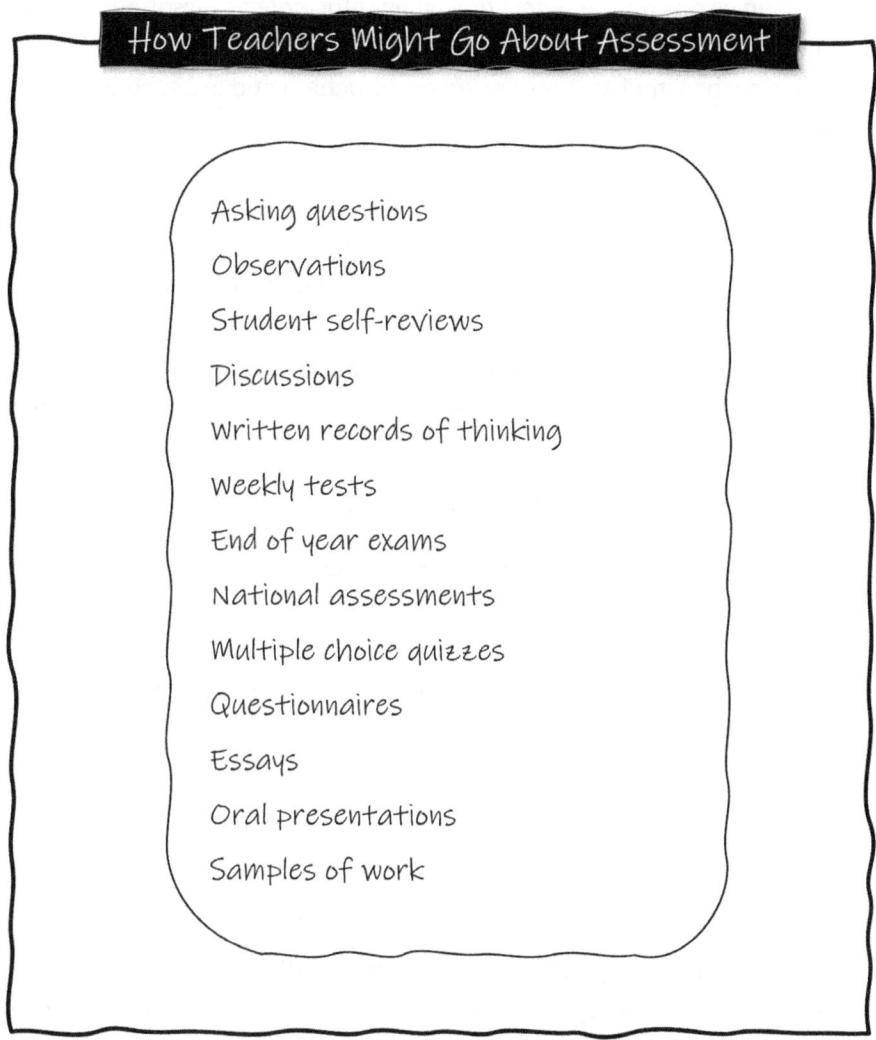

How Teachers Might Go About Assessment

Asking questions
Observations
Student self-reviews
Discussions
Written records of thinking
Weekly tests
End of year exams
National assessments
Multiple choice quizzes
Questionnaires
Essays
Oral presentations
Samples of work

Not all assessment is planned. Here are a few examples.

Conversations can take place during storytelling, while teachers read a book out loud to their students and when students are asked to read out loud. Effective teachers have learned how to question well; some also pre-plan questions, to direct at particular students. Notes might be taken after the reading.

There are many other times during the school day when informal conversations take place and when a question asked of one student becomes a learning opportunity for another. Teachers have no way of assessing every child in such instances. These incidental teaching and learning opportunities are often called 'Aha' moments.

A child might see the letters 'c-a-t' a dozen times before realising that the word 'cat' is made up of those three letters and sounds. Your children might be able to recite the seven times table but it could take some time before the groupings of sevens actually make sense and can be applied elsewhere.

This is all part of a typical school day. Not every teaching moment can be planned, and not everything planned can be taught as intended. Great teachers notice, build on and nurture these opportunities.

TEACHER JUDGEMENT

One of the major complaints teachers have is that schools have become overloaded with assessment tools, many of which overlap and aren't of great value.

Another problem is a lack of consistency in how teachers measure students' learning using *teacher judgement* – based on opinions.

Here's an example:
Student task: Write an opening paragraph to set the scene for your fiction text.

Student's paragraph:
Jackie entered the last door on the left-hand side of the long hallway on the third floor. The clock was still on the mantlepiece and the family portrait hanging above the clock was so much smaller than she remembered as a child. So many memories were made in this room and most of them were worth running away from. Why was she here? Did she do the right thing returning? Only time would tell.

Assessment:
Provides excellent detail in describing the scene (3 points)

Provides some detail in describing the scene. (2 points)

More detail is required to describe the scene. (1 point)

How would you assess the sample paragraph?

Chances are your judgement will not be the same as mine. The level of achievement in a task like this depends on a lot of things. The first is the intention of the task and what particular teaching points or learning has already taken place – think diagnostic, formative and summative tasks. What teaching has been done in preparation for the task and what is to follow? There are other considerations, including handwriting, reading and comprehension, and much more.

I've worked with hundreds of school leaders who struggle to get agreement on 'teacher judgements.' Not only does it cause frustration, it's also impossible. It comes back to our conversations about the value of a specified curriculum and the importance of a shared language of agreement.

If a more accurate measure of a student's technical ability in writing is required, a better alternative to the task just described would be a dictation test. Spelling, grammar and punctuation could then be assessed with accuracy.

Remember, make sure you know *what* is being assessed in every subject and *how*.

And make sure you find out *when* assessments are happening. This will help you help your children with time management if preparation and study are also required.

ASSESSING READING

I'd like to briefly touch on the assessment of reading as it's the most common and frequently assessed skill. Common reading assessments include three key components:

1. **Listening for accuracy.** Your children read out loud. The teacher listens for, and records, the number of words that are recognised and pronounced correctly.

2. **Listening for fluency.** Your children read out loud. The teacher listens for pace and other skills including tone, intonation, pausing and expression.

3. **Questioning for understanding.** Comprehension questions are often asked and other discussions or written responses might be required.

Can you identify which of these three components are qualitative and which are quantitative?

Because there is a combination of qualitative and quantitative measures, the outcome isn't always accurate.

Other problems can occur when schools use different programs or assessment tools – even across different year levels in the same school. This is largely due to choices about resources and assessment tools, mostly made at the individual school level. There is often confusion about how to use them properly, or assessment tools are seen as programs rather than resources. Problems are heightened by the differences in teachers' capability and knowledge about the teaching of reading.

Schools can wind up in an endless cycle of change. It can be easier to blame the product than do the necessary work of auditing a school's resources, including teacher capability.

The good news is that conversations about the teaching of phonics is now prompting more detailed discussions about teaching and assessment and greater consistency across schools.

The message here is that reading assessments don't look the same in all schools and, because reading happens right across the curriculum, it's really important to get assessments right.

ASSESSING TEACHERS

Guess what? Unlike students, teachers are not formally assessed.

To improve teacher performance, schools use a range of approaches, such as optional professional learning, peer observations, peer reviews and adjustments of teaching time.

For you, there's really no way of assessing teachers other than relying on communication, your gut feeling and what your children say about the teacher. And you don't have the luxury of choosing who teaches your children at school.

Some schools provide a parent questionnaire. It's more of an opinion survey prepared for all schools, not just yours. The focus is more on the home-school relationship rather than teacher quality.

If your assessment of the teaching staff isn't a good one, what options do you have?

You can say nothing at all. You can make a complaint (you'll have to familiarise yourself with the complaints process). Or you can change schools. Whichever option you choose, assessment will still come down to what your children have learned.

Until such time as we have more parents like you, who are committed to learning all you can about school education, formal assessment of teachers will pretty much remain out of bounds.

That's why your APLL groups are so important. You can work together to create change at a local level.

Homework

DO YOUR HOMEWORK.

Find out as much as you can about assessments in your children's classroom.

Use these questions as you do your research.

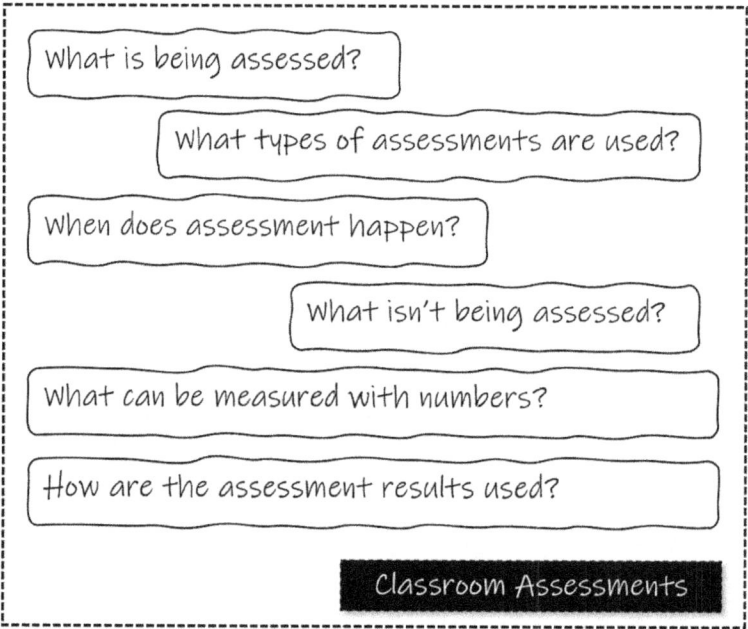

Family Time

TEACHING ABOUT ASSESSMENT

Ting struggled with oral presentations. Preparing the presentation was fine. Presenting in front of her peers was stressful. Helping her to address this by having her arrange a one-on-one with her teacher made all the difference.

Over a family meal, learn about how your children feel about different approaches being used in school and what strategies they are using to overcome any stressors.

If you have any stories about your experience of being assessed at school or work, be sure to share them.

APLL Group

WHAT DO YOU KNOW?

Here are a few topic starters as you discuss assessment.

> 1. How would you explain formative assessment?
> 2. What does a reading assessment capture?
> 3. Is a spelling test quantitative or qualitative?
> 4. What assessments does your classroom teacher use?
> 5. What are 3 questions you need to ask the classroom teacher about assessment?
>
> **Talking Assessment**

'Compare and contrast' is a common assessment method used in schools. Basically it helps to determine similarities and differences between things.

Here's an example:
The letters b and p are both made up of a straight line and a circle.

The letter b has a circle at the bottom of the straight line; p has a circle at the top.

If we added the letters q and d what would we compare and contrast?

Apply a 'compare and contrast' approach as you discuss the assessments that are happening in your children's classes. What's the same, similar or different? You'll get an idea about what's happening across the school.

That's a lot of great information for sharing, comparing and thinking about.

Learning Is Fun

One morning I walked into a classroom, just as a state-wide assessment was being conducted. Almost everything had been removed from the walls, except one poster at the back of the room. It read: *Learning Is Fun*. Directly underneath the poster sat a young girl, sobbing.

From the front of the room, the teacher was bellowing at the girl to stop crying and to start the test. The rest of the students tried to ignore the fiasco.

I walked over to the girl, knelt down beside her and asked her what was wrong. She told me her pencil was broken so she couldn't start the test. I felt sick to the stomach – for the little girl and for all the students who had witnessed what had happened. Something just didn't seem right. I decided to follow it up quietly.

It turned out that the teacher was a single mother of five children. She was on a teaching contract and had been told that morning she would lose her job if the students in her class didn't get good results.

With the support of the principal I helped her professionally and together we got her some counselling and family support.

And I continued to visit the class.

Things aren't always what they seem.

Wrap Up

- **LESSON 7:** Knowing what to measure, and how, is an essential principle of teaching and learning.

LESSON 8:
School Comes at a Cost

Another short history lesson.

The first public building in Melbourne, Australia, was paid for by donations of various denominations. It was to be used for services on Sabbath and Sundays and as a school during the week. A ship's bell summoned the children to school and citizens to worship.

Other local schoolhouses were built, often on land donated by wealthy families. The government would contribute to the cost of construction of the schoolhouse.

Communities now had a place for children to be *schooled* and the local committee charged with overseeing the schoolhouse could approve of its use for any other community purpose.

The community also employed its own teachers, who first had to pass government exams. They could then deliver the agreed specified curriculum and receive a salary. All schoolhouses, regardless of location, offered the same *non-negotiable specified curriculum*.

Parents could pay for extra subjects offered. This fee would cover the cost of the teacher, including bonuses based on pupil's results in the specified curriculum. These extra subjects weren't always the same in every school.

Free, compulsory and secular education is still here today. There's still local community decision making too. Its authority could still be just as strong. It just requires energy from parents like you.

WATCH THE LANGUAGE

It's always important to address any words or ideas that cause confusion.

Take the word 'free'. When discussing 'free, compulsory and secular education', what does 'free' mean? Some options are: at no charge; those involved may do as they please; or all restrictions are removed.

I'm not sure any of these apply. Let's explore the options.

'At no charge'. What might have been considered 'free' for children from homes with little means was paid for by families with the means, who covered their costs. This still applies today. The difference is that the cost of schooling is no longer paid directly from your pocket to the school. It's distributed by the government through your taxes. Nothing comes free.

'Those involved may do as they please' or 'all restrictions are removed'. You know that schools have rules or policies tied to the laws of society. And you know that the reason for a school's existence is to give every child an equal opportunity to receive an agreed education. With responsibility, freedom follows. Without it, society would not function.

So, what does 'free' mean concerning school education?

If you've chosen to have your children educated in a non-government school, the concept of user pays (via school fees) applies. If you don't pay, your children can no longer attend.

For families who choose to send their children to a state government school, the concept of a voluntary contribution applies – you're not obliged to make that payment. Your children can still attend.

Here's the catch. All schools receive a government contribution towards instruction. The more families contribute themselves the better the resources and the greater the educational options.

What about 'compulsory'?

It's a self-explanatory term that means something is required by law or an obligation. What comes to mind is attending school and attending schooling. If school attendance is required by law, there wouldn't be the option of home-schooling, hospital schools or schools of the air. Could it be that compulsory is more related to being taught a curriculum rather than physically attending a particular place?

I suspect it is a combination of the two. History would teach us a lot here don't you think?

Lastly, let's look at 'secular'.

Here's what I've explored in one dictionary:

- Relating to worldly or temporal (time-related) matters
- Not specifically religious.

Here's a statement I found.
The word 'secular' is primarily used to distinguish something, such as an attitude, belief or position, that is not specifically religious in nature.

How would you describe free, compulsory and secular education?

When considering your answer, keep in mind the different types of schools available including state government, non-government and religious schools. You might want to think about needs and wants too.

'Free, compulsory and secular education' is fairly familiar as a phrase. It seems that understanding what it means for your family isn't quite so simple.

ESSENTIAL ITEMS

There has long been an understanding that *essential items* your child needs for school are provided.

Here's an example from a departmental website.
Schools provide students with free instruction and ensure students have free access to all items, activities and services that are used by the school to fulfil the standard curriculum requirements.

Does this make sense to you?

I understand the statement to mean resources are available in schools for instruction or teaching. (teachers are also a resource) Your children have access to these. The items your children need for learning, however, are *not free*.

I bet you have accepted requests from schools to purchase particular items – usually from stationery and book lists. And you'd be right in doing so. It comes back to responsibility. *Nothing comes free of charge.*

Oh, and did you notice the word *standard*. It's pretty clear a *specified curriculum* doesn't exist. So, if that's not clear, no wonder there's always confusion about curriculum, funding and the increasing cost of sending your children to school.

OUT OF SCHOOL EXPENSES

Putting your budget aside, deciding how much to spend on your children's school education depends on what you expect to get for your money. You might value the culture and history, or the range of opportunities a particular non-government school offers.

Even if you can afford a non-government school, you might prefer your children to attend the local government school. Your children would then learn alongside their neighbourhood friends.

Other circumstances, including location or family circumstances, might affect your choices.

Just remember that education is life-long. Schools can't and won't provide every educational experience that your children need or want. Don't be persuaded to spend money on something offered at school when there are better options elsewhere.

There will always be additional expenses related to your children's interests, health and general education, regardless of the school your children attend or how much you invest with the school.

FUNDING SAMENESS AND DIFFERENCE

While it's fair to say the funding formula is complex, all financial contributions, grants and budget allocation is no different in schools than in any other business or service provider. It must be managed well.

Without going into detail, there's a national formula used to agree on the cost to the government for each child's school education. Schools submit enrolment information about your child and in return the school receives the funding; you don't.

The formula also includes the allocation of additional government funding a school receives for individual students. Criteria for this extra funding include students living with disability, and students from families where languages other than English are spoken at home. Of great concern is there isn't extra funding for students who are gifted and talented.

Clearly there are differences in student capabilities and needs. It seems to me there is a dreadful mismatch between funding and need.

You know that you cannot meet every educational need your child has. Neither can the school.

All families have diverse abilities to meet children's needs. So do schools. In spite of this, funding contributions seem to be one sided. All funding goes to the schools, and they decide how it is spent. Not only does your family miss out, so do other service providers and professionals, who might be able to bridge the gaps the schools cannot fill.

THE INEQUALITY FUNDING DEBATE

The reporting of inequality and the need for more funding in schools is often in the media. It might lead you to believe that children in state government schools are somehow worse off than children in non-government schools. It seems asking for money has become the stock standard solution. *Spend more and schools will offer greater value.* Don't accept this blindly.

First of all, school funding is a nightmare to understand and comparisons between private schools and government public schools make little sense. It's like comparing a family that goes on holiday to Europe with a family who holidays at a local campsite. We don't know the family details and can only make assumptions. All we can say confidently is that families are entitled to take a holiday.

The real inequality in school education affects everyone equally. And it is this: we don't have a specified curriculum.

When schools don't begin with a specified curriculum, delivered by capable teachers, there is no way of accurately measuring the value of anything in school education. And that includes funding and grants, school fees and voluntary contributions.

That's the inequality debate you need to lead.

Homework

MAPPING THEIR LEARNING

Make a list of expenses related to your children's education which are not included in the initial fees or contributions you make to their schooling.

Here are some categories to get you started.

> In school extras
> Out of school interests
> Travel expenses (including drop off and pick up)
> Educational experiences during vacation
> Before and after school care
> Family experiences
> Birthday parties with an educational twist
> Fees and essential items
> Uniforms and extras
>
> **Education Costs**

Review your list, add to it and calculate your expenses.

Another valuable exercise is to look for duplication and opportunities for cost cutting.

Family Time

POCKET MONEY

Here's a simple way to invest some money in your children's learning – other than at school.

Set these three rules:

1. School work must not be included in 'jobs' to be done
2. Pocket money must not be spent at school
3. Bonuses cannot be related to schoolwork.

How to get started:
Decide on a base value. Just for argument's sake, let's say it's $1

When your children begin school, they receive $1 pocket money per week for doing agreed jobs around the house.

For every birthday you add an extra 50 cents to their weekly stipend.

> Let's say you have two school aged children – a five-year-old and an eight-year-old. The five-year-old will collect $1 every week until her next birthday, at which time her pocket money will be adjusted to $1.50 per week. The eight-year-old will collect $2.50 per week until his ninth birthday, at which time a 50-cent adjustment will mean $3.00 weekly.
> They can save, donate or spend their money in any way other than on anything connected to the school.
> Feel free to adjust the $ value to suit your financial situation.
>
> **Pocket Change**

APLL Group

REACHING OUT FOR RESEARCH

Time for a little homework on school funding.

Here's a list of queries. Share them between you and report back at your next catch up.

1. What are our school fees or expected voluntary contributions?
2. Are costs to parents easy to find and understand?
3. How much does the government contribute to the school's budget?
4. What are the school policies on funding, fundraising and parent payments?
5. How does school funding from government work?
6. What is the avenue for community discussion about funding and fees?
7. What is the school budget?
8. What are the fundraising priorities?
9. What are the greatest costs to the school?
10. How can we be better educated on school funding?

School Funding

Double Dip and Sacrifice

Between them, my two girls have attended 10 schools. Some moves have been because of my vocation and living overseas; others have been due to other circumstances. Sze Ting also spent a short period of time in home schooling when she was between schools.

When she was in the first grade Ting was invited to try out for an international gymnastics squad. She was successful. It was extremely exciting for her but came with many challenges. Family life changed overnight.

Chauffeuring her between the gymnastics club, school and home meant there were changes in family income, a stretched budget, fewer family holidays and less time spent with Somraudee. The greatest challenge was balancing this new life with Ting's school education.

Her gymnastics career lasted 7 years and spanned three of the six schools she attended. One was a non-government secondary school. Enrolment included compulsory Saturday morning sport but, as she was already juggling gymnastics with school demands, compulsory sport wasn't possible for her.

Despite that, Saturday sport came with the cost of non-government school fees, as did access to the rowing club, state of the art theatre and more. These facilities were all very impressive but they were of no benefit or interest to Ting while she was doing gymnastics elsewhere.

If there was a 'user pays' opportunity, the cost of extras could have been deducted from the school fees.

That wasn't to be. It was a case of double dip and sacrifice for a number of years.

Wrap Up

- **LESSON 8:** Funding a non-negotiable specified curriculum and honouring diverse abilities can remove school inequality.

LESSON 9:
Big Tech, Little Tech

Your children have grown up with devices. Depending on your age and how you earn a living, you've also had ample time to become familiar with them and potentially to become dependent on them.

Devices and their use in schools is a sticking point. Teachers love them, loathe them or just live with them. You're probably much the same.

I have a love-hate relationship with devices in schools. It began at Teacher's College, in 1982 – the same year Microsoft developed the first PC-compatible mouse, which evolved from the first trackball invented in 1946. In fact, I've just learned about the trackball while writing this book.

Anyway, by the time I hit the classroom running I was using the Apple IIE. There was no coding in the curriculum, schools generally had one computer to share between multiple staff, and the computer was mainly used for desktop publishing.

Your knowledge and interest in information technology might well be entirely different from mine. Chances are your views on technology in schools will be different from those of other parents and some teachers as well.

It's been a few decades since my first year of teaching, and technology has come a long way but, to be frank, I'm still dead against 'a device for every child in primary school'.

Being open about my views on Information Technology (IT) has landed me in all sorts of strife. It hasn't stopped me, though, from saying what I believe.

What do you think? Is IT in your children's school your business?

INFORMATION TECHNOLOGY BEYOND NOW

I'm curious to know whether or not you see yourself as tech savvy, and whether you think your children's teachers are.

Here's what I see from my vantage point.

Information technology (IT) is moving at such a rapid pace that schools can't keep up. Some schools have introduced departments dedicated solely to the management of devices; others employ a non-teaching IT specialist. Many promote one of their teachers to an IT specialist role. This promotion isn't based on technological expertise; the teacher just happens to be the one with most knowledge and confidence.

You can imagine the difference between schools when it comes to understanding IT.

What you might not realise is that *technological understanding* has been an educational priority since 1988, yet teachers – including those promoted to IT positions – have never been required to boost their qualifications in this area.

Great teachers with a talent for technology aren't sufficiently recognised and utilised and teachers with only a general understanding are missing out on what could be a valuable career opportunity.

Where does this leave your children?

Unless your children attend a pencil-free and paperless school, chances are IT as a discipline isn't being taught sufficiently well.

Start to separate what your children *can* do with information technology from what they *need* to do with it. Ask how it affects their learning. Investigate exactly how and why devices are being used as tools across the curriculum. Read up on technology as a discipline.

And don't forget to keep track of trends and new developments, such as 3D printing and Artificial Intelligence.

Ultimately, you should be asking yourself, 'Are these resources essential for my children's education at this point in time?' If so, start thinking of them as teaching essentials and find out how they're being used.

FACT AND OPINION

Devices aren't automatic substitutes for books. Learning how to research must still include learning how to use a library. Then there must be learning about how to select the right research material and to distinguish between fact and opinion.

How well does your school teach these skills?

An Internet search on any topic can result in millions of 'hits' (sources of information) and chances are you've been caught out confusing fact and fiction. We all have. Imagine what this means for your children.

A quick reminder: devices are resources – that's all. Are they essential for learning at school?

CYBER SECURITY AND OWNERSHIP

Let's look now at cyber security.

When was the last time you read the fine print before signing up for a new app or purchasing new software? There's just so much to read. We've become accustomed to ticking the boxes without thinking about the consequences; schools are doing the same thing.

In exchange for access to many of the apps and programs recommended by your children's school, private information is collected. And, because some schools take out licensing agreements and then invite you to sign up, schools are passing on your personal information as part of the agreement, without your explicit consent.

To make matters worse, some of these licensing agreements allow overseas companies to access and share your details. You *must* read the fine print. Don't compromise your security.

Identity theft has costly consequences. You don't want this to happen.

Imagine taking your 18-year-old to secure a loan for her first car, only to learn of massive debts racked up in her name, through software recommended by schools. This is happening. Believe me. And guess what? There would be nothing you could do about it. You signed up and you ticked the box.

Add to that the hundreds of thousands of child abuse files that have been intercepted, containing material accessed via software recommended by schools, to which parents had consented.

Go ahead and try new programs and follow the latest trends. It's not my place to stop you. Just please don't compromise your security or your children's position in the process.

Making your own decisions without being controlled by anybody else is something to be proud of. This is taking ownership. It's acting responsibly. Don't be coerced or made to feel like a bad parent for asserting your right to be in control of your own decisions. And don't apologise for being frank, for asking questions or saying 'no' to digital devices, apps and software.

Your children are *your* children. Their education is your responsibility and, last time I looked, devices weren't essential items. How could they be when there's no specified curriculum aligned with their use.

TRANSFORMATION AND THE BASICS

There's no doubt we've made progress. The speed at which we moved from switchboards and dial up phones to push button and cordless phones was extraordinary. Now there are smart phones and smart watches.

Your children will experience far greater technological change in their lifetimes than we could possibly imagine.

But guess what? Even the simplest of technological tasks still requires an understanding of the fundamentals or basics in English and Mathematics. To call people, we still need to read the numerals 0-9 and the letters that represent their names. If you want spelling and mathematical accuracy, you can't rely entirely on a spell check or a calculator.

Reading, writing and arithmetic are as important today as they were centuries ago. If your children aren't learning these skills properly, what on earth are they doing with devices in primary school? And what is the impact on their learning when they get to secondary school.

I'll be frank: if your children can't read a map, spell accurately to an agreed standard without spell check or apply mathematical concepts without a calculator and have no known barriers to learning, perhaps there needs to be a rethink about devices. And perhaps you need to be frank too!

Homework

GETTING FROM A TO B

When your children begin to drive, could they get to their destination without Siri, Google and friends? Do they know how to read a map?

Take a trip to the local library with your children, providing directions.

When you get there, watch how they search for information on a topic that interests them.

If your children have their own device for school use and have difficulty with either of these two tasks, it's something to raise with their teachers. Find out what is being taught.

Learn how your children are taught to research information at the school library before researching on devices.

Family Time

TIME FOR A SECURITY CHECK

Of course your children have on-screen leisure time. I'm sure you manage that properly. Then there's what happens at school.

Have you ever wondered how much of the screen time they have at home is a result of demands made by the school? That could be worth monitoring.

You should also consider the issue of security. Online classes and group chats are relatively easy for you to manage in your home. You might need to do some further exploration into the security issues relating to apps and software you have installed at the request of your children's school.

Here's a way to get started.

> How many box ticking requests from your children's school have you had?
> 1. Make a list of apps and software
> 2. Check the app or program for account and profile details
> 3. Identify if you signed up or if the school did so on your behalf
> 4. How often is the app or program being used? Are you getting value for money?
> 5. List any questions you have for the teacher about why the app or program is needed
> 6. Choose to opt out or stay in
>
> HINT: If anything appears to be a substitute for teaching, be sure to add this to the list of questions for the teacher.
>
> **Security Check**

APLL Group

CONSIDER THIS!

When you think about it, schools are ideal places for collecting all sorts of information about your family. And, with the use of devices and apps, it seems they've become pretty good tracking and research hubs too.

Surely this isn't what schools are about.

If your children practise their 'times tables' on an app, for example, what personal details about your or your children are required?

To help your children learn their times tables, what options, other than technology, can you think of?

Replace 'their times tables' with learning in other knowledge or topic areas and share what ideas you can come up with. You might be able to help each other to reduce screen time and app time for your children and resolve the privacy dilemma.

The Digital Divide

Are you familiar with the Digital Education Revolution (DER) in Australia? It started in 2007. Secondary schools were promised one computer for every student. The Federal Government promised to pay for them.

Even though the DER didn't include primary schools, the principal and school council at Ting's school wanted to introduce one computer for every child.

A group of parents, including me, met to discuss the proposal. There were various viewpoints, which was a good thing. We all learned a great deal. Even parents who were fully supportive of the idea had concerns, including the cost of computers, Internet access and battery charging, furniture, the weight of backpacks, eye strain and screen time. There were dozens of other concerns.

These concerns and viewpoints were collated and given to the school board.

The school leadership then held an information session. One important fact was *not* shared: *a computer device is not an essential item.*

When the school leadership was asked about it, everything changed. No further questions were allowed. Parents were ushered to tables to sign a lease agreement for their children to use a device.

Parents were told that unless they signed up for the computer lease agreement, their children would be disadvantaged.

The community was divided and the issue escalated. I won't go into details, except to say that the DER has been a complete sham. If computer devices were considered a necessary teaching item, every school would ensure every student had access to one – at school – at no cost to parents. The computers would also be upgraded on a regular basis, also at no extra cost to families.

The cost and accountability for devices and the implications for families have all been transferred to school parents – including you.

Wrap Up

- **LESSON 9:** Electronic devices are not essential for learning.

LESSON 10:
School Days

Summer school is available in schools in the US. It is a targeted program designed to help children achieving below the expected standard in English and/or Mathematics to catch up. If they pass summer school, they can avoid repeating the entire previous school year.

In preparation for a new position I had accepted in New York, I was asked to fly over and consult for six weeks in the summer school program. My work included coaching elementary school principals and delivering professional development.

Summer school classes were taught by teachers already employed at the school. For them it was a short-term contracted second job – a bonus income. For the children, it was a second chance.

For me, it was an eye opener – an opportunity to see school buildings used productively during the vacation.

Schools in Australia don't offer this program. Schools are closed for instruction every term holiday. Some schools offer holiday programs but they are not run by the school's teachers. It's a 'user pays' system.

Today, there are just over 9,500 schools in Australia and almost 296,000 full time teachers. With all those schools closed for 12 weeks every year, that's an enormous waste of valuable resources.

When I was teaching, I took for granted that my job came with 12 weeks leave every school year. I never once questioned the closing of schools. Neither did any of my colleagues and friends or any of my students' parents. Closing schools for at least 12 weeks every year was, and still is, just the way things are.

What do you think?

THE 40/12 PRINCIPLE

Are you ready to be bombarded with questions? Here goes!

What does your calendar year look like? Are you like the thousands of families who struggle to coordinate work and family life with the school calendar?

I call it the 40/12 principle. 40 weeks under instruction and 12 weeks over budget.

Some couples don't have children. Some families rely on one income and others, two. The logistics of school, work and family life differ. For the hundreds of thousands of single, divorced or separated parents, whether in full-time or shared parenting roles, work and family life can be incredibly stressful. And let's not forget shift workers. To live and work around school life can be difficult.

Many businesses struggle, too. There aren't always creative ways to work around employee needs without reducing profit. If you're a business owner, you have the added problem of juggling a business and its employees' needs and your own family needs.

If you are managing an extra workload beyond your home duties, what are your options? If your annual leave doesn't coincide with school holidays, what can you do? Do you call on grandparents? Do you have out of pocket expenses for holiday programs?

What are the arrangements you are currently making?

THE SCHOOL DAY

The difficulty you and all other school parents must deal with is how best to arrange your family life around school hours. Juggling family life isn't just a school holiday problem.

Here's the catch. Generally, children are of compulsory school age from ages 5 to 16. They will begin school at around 9:00 am and finish at 3:30 pm and follow this routine for 40 weeks of the calendar year. You're expected to make family decisions based on this routine for 11 years with the option of 2 more senior years. Add the 12-week holiday period and boom! Welcome to the dictatorship of an inflexible school system over family life. And we have all come to accept it.

IT'S JUST THE WAY THINGS ARE

Here's a common dilemma:
Your workday commence at 8:30 am and ends at 5.00 pm. School commences at 9:00 am and ends at 3.00 pm. You have a 5-minute commute between home and school and a 1-hour commute between school and work. You have a 2 hour commute every day and you spend 2.5 hours more at work than your children do at school.

Working around school hours can be problematic.

What are your options?

- Leave things as they are
- Work less and earn less
- Rely on the support of someone else for school drop off and pick up
- Pay for before and after school care or child minding
- Stop paid work and be there for your children's school life.

Are these options reasonable?

TEACHING AND LEARNING HOURS

You might be wondering about the position of educators, especially those who are also parents.

School teachers fit into the same category as most full-time employees. They are employed to work no more than a 38-hour week and are entitled to four weeks annual leave.

Of those 38-hours worked, teachers cannot teach any more than 22 hours per week. The remaining 16 hours are spent on things other than teaching.

Back to the scenario and your children.

- Your children are in class for 25 hours per week
- Your family spends 22.5 hours a week juggling home-work-school and family life

- Teachers are in class for 22 hours per week
- Teachers can leave the school premises 15 minutes after the school day ends

What do you expect from schools in return for juggling your family life around school hours for 11 or 13 years?

In fact, the problem isn't limited to school families. The school calendar dictates other aspects of your life. Think about the congestion on the roads on school days. School holidays are considered peak periods for travel, costing your family more. And, as the population grows, taxpayer funds are spent on the construction of more schools that will sit empty for at least 3 months of the year.

Is this as bad as it gets?

HEART STRINGS

Working conditions for teachers are signed off by unions and employers. Even teachers not in a union are bound by these negotiations. And, like any who have employment agreements, teachers have duties and entitlements.

Their employment conditions have a direct day to day impact on your children and your family. Very little, if anything, about this is reported but there are plenty of reports about how difficult work and life are for teachers.

Here are some examples:

- As many as 80% of teachers work an average of 53 hours per week
- More than half the teacher workforce suffers from stress and mental health problems
- Teacher stress levels are caused by 'helicopter' parents and aggressive parents.

It seems teacher unions aren't representing their members; employers and school boards are ignoring occupational health and safety matters and teachers with children are also struggling with home-school-work and family life difficulties. This has a direct impact on your children.

There's also regular reporting about teachers working an average 15 hours of unpaid overtime every week. Would you work 15 hours overtime without pay, week after week, year after year?

I bet you wouldn't – unless there were benefits. It seems, in the case of teachers, there are. Teachers are not required to attend their workplace when instruction is not taking place. That means, during the 12 weeks that schools are closed, teachers can take holidays. Who really knows whether they have worked overtime or not?

Essentially, for every week teachers claim to do 15 hours overtime, they have two days of leave – two days where you have to make adjustments, including financial ones. You are relinquishing a healthier home-school-work and family life blend for you and your family.

On the other hand, there are teachers who really do work an average of 53 hours per week and are stressed because they are cramming a 48-week work year into 40 weeks. This is having an impact on your children as well.

It seems that either way, our current system does not favour family life.

100 DAYS OF SCHOOL: WHOSE HOMEWORK?

In the northern hemisphere, schools celebrate 100 days of school. Children are given a homework task to make a poster with 100 items.

The work handed in ranges from the most extraordinary and expensive 3D artwork to 100 cotton balls pasted on poster board. Over time, 100 days of school has gone from a celebration and counting exercise for children to a homework task for parents, who compete to prove their own wealth and creativity.

Homework given by schools adds to the already busy lives of families. It's of major concern that homework tasks and the approximate time and cost required to complete them are not sufficiently considered.

Homework takes time away from families, from children's other learning opportunities and from their social life and 'down time'. It can become another home-school-work and family life nightmare.

Homework has value if set for these three reasons:

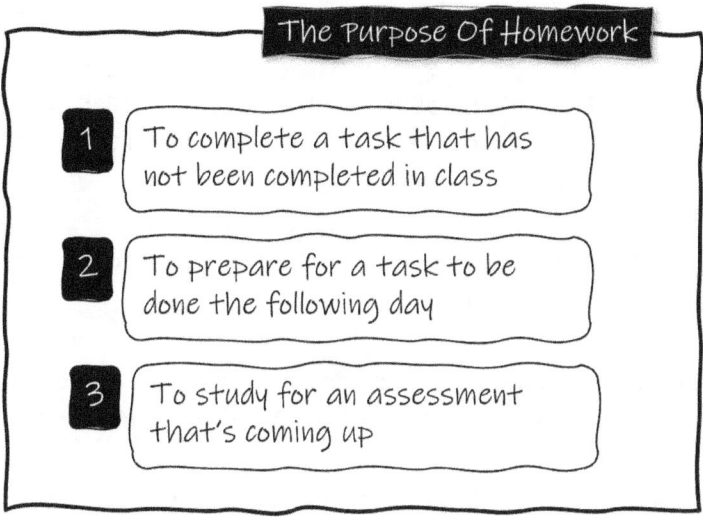

The Purpose Of Homework
1. To complete a task that has not been completed in class
2. To prepare for a task to be done the following day
3. To study for an assessment that's coming up

Homework isn't for parents to do and should *never* be a substitute for teaching.

WHO COMES FIRST?

If you had to choose between feeding your own children or making sure other parents could feed theirs, which would it be?

You might think there are only two possible answers but there are three. The third option is that you feed your own children while doing all you can to help other parents feed theirs.

A teacher's working life is spent doing things that affect your children. The appropriate professional approach is to act in your children's best interests.

But what if teachers are also parents and your children's best interests are in conflict with the best interests of their own children?

The annual school calendar – the 40/12 principle – highlights this conflict.

To work a 38-hour week and have 4-weeks annual leave would compromise the flexibility currently enjoyed by teachers who are also parents. And, for teachers who are not parents, the loss of flexibility is just as great.

Every day teachers make decisions about your children. Every day their decisions fall somewhere between what's best for your children and what's best for their job security and, if they are parents, for their own children.

The current 40/12 principle is causing havoc in your children's education, your family life and the wellbeing of teachers. Let's do something about it.

What if schools were open for instruction 12 hours a day, for 52 weeks of the year and all school families, including teachers, had flexibility over attendance and holiday arrangements?

Would that make a difference to your family time, budget and everyone's wellbeing?

I believe it would.

Homework

IT'S THEIR HOMEWORK

A word of advice.

When your children are given homework and they ask for help, find out what type of help they need. You'll usually get one of these three answers:

They don't understand what's being asked of them

They have run out of time and are in a panic

They can't be bothered doing the homework and are pulling on your heartstrings.

These are my suggestions in each case.

> Here are my suggestions:
>
> 1. Speak to the teacher. Explain that your children need to be taught what they don't yet understand
> 2. Use this as the ideal opportunity to make some changes to routines at home. It might mean less TV or computer time
> 3. Don't cave in. I get it. I've been there. I'm guilty too. But if you do, you've done the work and your children haven't learned a thing
>
> **Managing Homework**

Family Time

QUALITY OVER QUANTITY

It's so easy to get caught up in our own responsibilities and distractions.

At present you can't control the school day. The great news is that school cannot control your family time. That's for you to determine. You are like everyone else; you cannot buy more time, give it away or waste it. You are always doing something. See what you can do to create more quality in family time rather than panic over lack of quantity.

Here are five ideas to get started:

1. Make a map of the everyone's weekday and highlight the times you have together
2. Have dinner together at the table
3. Turn off the TV often
4. Start your own family audio book club
5. Go for regular walks

Quality Family Time

APLL Group

CHECK IN ON HOME AND WORK

Schools send out questionnaires that are often generic or tailored to a decision already made by the school. It's time to turn the tables.

You already know that home-school-work and family life is compromised by the current structure of the school day.

What can you do?

1. Learn about the challenges facing other parents

2. Share your findings with your group and, based on the results, create a list of possible solutions

3. Host an APLL event and present the findings and solutions to parents

4. Elect representatives to present the information to the school board

5. Ask that it be distributed to families, including teachers, to begin a healthy movement for change.

If your school has a Parents Association (PA), it already has a direct link to the school board and is answerable to it. Consider working with the PA without relinquishing your independence.

No Ideal School for Ting

By Year 4, Ting's gymnastics training commitments totalled 26 hours per week. By the time she reached secondary school, her training schedule had increased to 30 hours per week.

These hours were spread across five days. On four days, there were split sessions, when she would have training from 7.00 am to 10.00 am, then school, followed by a second training session in the late afternoon and evening.

Ting's gymnastics training was about developing discipline, motivation, self-esteem, grit, teamwork and a profound regard for her peers. She dreamed of competing in the Olympic Games.

As for school, there were two options: reconsider home schooling or juggle school and training. I needed to earn an income, so we juggled.

During primary school, Ting's gym and school schedules were much easier to manage. When she started secondary school, she was expected to complete the same workload as every full-time student. It also became clear she needed tutoring to catch up on the mathematics she had missed in primary school, on top of her 30 hours per week training schedule.

For 7 years, I negotiated with her schools. Extensions for assignments were granted, absence from classes was not counted as non-attendance and, on rare occasions, there was a reduction in the number of repetitive assessment tasks she was required to complete.

Although these negotiations were of some help, there were still two fundamental, and unresolved, problems:

1. There was no option to reduce the number of subjects for study. All subjects required work to be completed, despite Ting's non-attendance
2. Regardless of the shorter time Ting attended school, the full financial contribution from the government went directly to the school.

Three things would have made all the difference:

1. Government funding for Ting's school education given to the service provider of our choice
2. Flexible school hours
3. More education service providers, other than schools, who could offer a specified curriculum.

This would have enabled two options:

Option 1: School and Gym
The school would receive funding for essential subjects including English and Mathematics. The gym would receive funding for the teaching of Gymnastics and associated Health and Physical Education. Ting would attend both venues.

Option 2: Gym
The gym would receive all the government allocated funding and employ staff to teach subjects including English and Mathematics in between training. Ting would only have to attend one venue.

Wrap Up

- **LESSON 10**: Families make adjustments to home-school-work and family life fit around inflexible school hours.

LEARNINGS FROM PART 2:
Lessons From The Classroom

LESSON 1: A school's philosophy should be easy to understand. It should respect your right to fulfil your responsibility for your children's education and your children's right to have your protection.

LESSON 2: Schools and teachers can value different approaches to teaching and learning.

LESSON 3: A university teaching degree isn't a licence to teach anything to anyone.

LESSON 4: There are different types of curriculum.

LESSON 5: Being literate means being able to produce, understand and use English to interact in the right way with anyone.

LESSON 6: A non-negotiable specified curriculum can sit alongside negotiable electives and other education services.

LESSON 7: Knowing what to measure, and how, is an essential principle of teaching and learning.

LESSON 8: Funding a non-negotiable specified curriculum and honouring diverse abilities can remove school inequality.

LESSON 9: Electronic devices are not essential for learning.

LESSON 10: Families make adjustments to home-schoolwork and family life, to fit around inflexible school hours.

Part 3:
Lessons From The Boardroom

Lessons From The Boardroom

1. Country-Wide Local Schools

2. Ownership and Collaboration

3. Strategy and Change

4. Education Services

Boardrooms. There's still so much to learn. Even though that's true, chances are you don't realise the enormity of what you already knew, how much you've learned, and what you can teach others.

Let me explain.

What you know about family and school life is more than what I knew as a first-time mum. What you'll soon learn about school boards will be more than I knew as a first-year teacher. You are in a very strong position.

What you're about to discover is the value of your relationship with your local school board. With your insights and growing knowledge and a strong parent network, you can support your school board to say 'no' to mediocre school education and 'yes' to being a *School of Distinction™*.

What's a School of Distinction™?

You already know the answer; you just don't know that you know!

More about that shortly.

Meanwhile, brace yourself for the last leg of your journey.

Just one more thing. Now you're looking into, and perhaps out from, the school board level, in Part 3, the Homework and Family Time activities are entirely yours to determine. You'll still *see* suggestions for your Australian Parents Leading Learning group.

Have fun!

LESSON 1:
Country Wide Local Schools

Every school family is a part of its school community. A local school community includes parents, students and staff of the school and other people who have a connection with it.

The snippets of history and lessons you have read offer some insights into the similarities and differences among school communities.

Here's a few we have explored:

- Australian law and school rules are based on Judaeo-Christian values. Some families follow other faiths, too

- The community includes nuclear families, where mum, dad and their offspring live together, but there are many other different family groupings

- English is Australia's common language. Other languages are spoken in many family homes and some people speak more than two languages

- People have the same fundamental needs. They have different interests and diverse abilities

- Some parents are actively involved in schools; others are not

- Schools offer the same subjects. Not all teachers, however, have the same subject knowledge

- Governments contribute to the cost of teaching; families meet the cost of learning

- Schools follow the standard Australian Curriculum, which is adapted many times at different levels. There is no longer a specified curriculum.

School education is emotional. It must be. It involves communities of people and people are emotional. Thankfully, people are also rational.

Even so, when dealing with different views or positions like those on the list above, we tend to fall back on emotion. For example, you will feel much safer if you avoid speaking up in front of others, because you're afraid you'll blush. Your fallback position is to see through your emotional lens and act accordingly. You end up not making a rational contribution.

Other tendencies we've talked are to have blind faith in education, and to view it through your childhood lens. This won't happen in your case anymore but it still happens in schools and at school board meetings all over the country.

Trust me when I say there is nothing to fear about school boards. That's a message to spread far and wide.

YOUR SCHOOL BOARD

Your school board serves your school community in a variety of ways. Board members listen to ideas about improving learning and teaching. They aim to agree on the philosophy, vision and mission of the school. They make decisions about how school resources are used for current and future education services. Your school board is the voice of your school community.

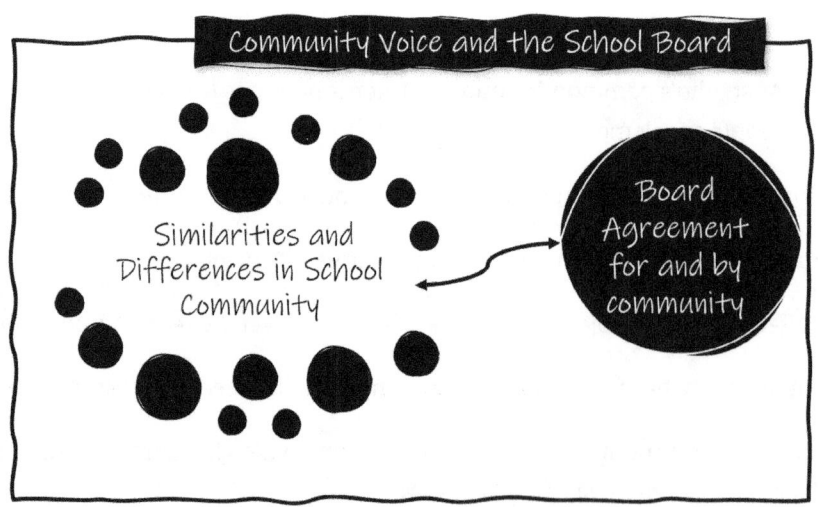

The board also forms sub-committees to work towards achieving specific goals. Members of the school community can join sub-committees without having to be members of the board.

Every year, members are elected to your school board. It's a formal process, just like any other election. Your school website should have details of the process. The election is advertised, allowing ample time for people to put their names forward as candidates.

Parent, teacher, and community representatives are elected and, in some schools, there are also student representatives on the board.

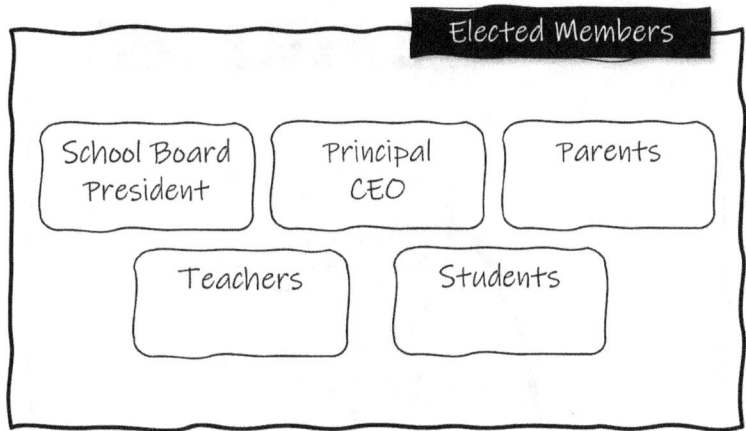

If your school board doesn't hold elections, it means board members are selected. If this is the case, you should find out who chooses the board members and what their reasons are for opting for 'selection' rather than 'election'.

I don't want to sound cynical but, unless there is good reason, such as a very small school community, you want to be sure everything is above board. It has been known for principals to choose people based on favouritism, protectionism and vested interests, rather than do what is right for the school community.

TOP-DOWN, BOTTOM-UP

Your school board is part of a top-down bottom-up decision-making process. This is a process where the 'big picture' goals of the organisation are made at the top and the finer details of what's needed to achieve those goals come from the bottom up.

There are several layers of top-down bottom-up relationships across the entire school system. The lowest layer is the relationship between your children and their teachers. The highest is between the school board and the Federal Government. The school board is the link between your family and your country's big picture school education goals.

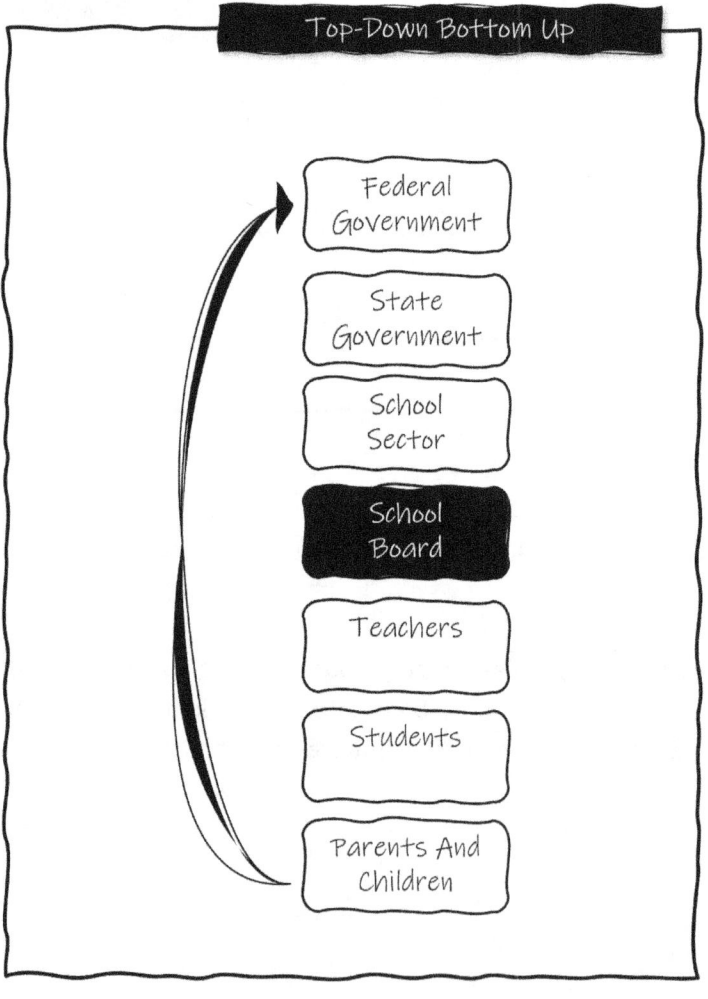

If something is affecting your children, chances are it is also affecting other children. When you do what's right for your own children, you boost the confidence of other parents to do the same for theirs.

There's another lesson here. Because you are responsible for your children's school education, you hold the leading position in both top-down and bottom-up processes.

It doesn't matter whether or not you become an active member of the board, or of any committees. You need to know what's currently going on and what the future holds for the school. This information should be readily available.

BOARD COMPOSITION

The composition of the school board is something else to think about.

Let's say there are 15 members of the board: 7 parent representatives; 6 school staff representatives (including the principal); and 4 community members.

All 6 staff are members of a teachers' union and only 2 have children. Of the 7 parents, 2 are lawyers, 3 are at-home parents and the other 2 are government employees. Three of the community members have older children who used to attend the school; one is a friend of the principal.

Here's why I want you to think about this. If these people were 'selected', community representation could fall a number of ways – for instance, full support of the community or loyalty to the principal, union and government.

A better way of looking at the composition is to take out any emotion and think rationally. From a top-down and bottom-up perspective, who are the influencers and decision makers?

The 'parent vs teacher' narrative is dreadful for everyone. Those who represent you are parents and professionals. If parents are seen as parents who also wear their 'professional' hats, teachers should be viewed in the same way. Different vantage points are then wide open for discussion and vested interests can be identified.

A 'parent vs teacher' mentality can be stamped out by the school board in a heartbeat and you can help make it happen.

APLL Group

CHARTING YOUR SCHOOL

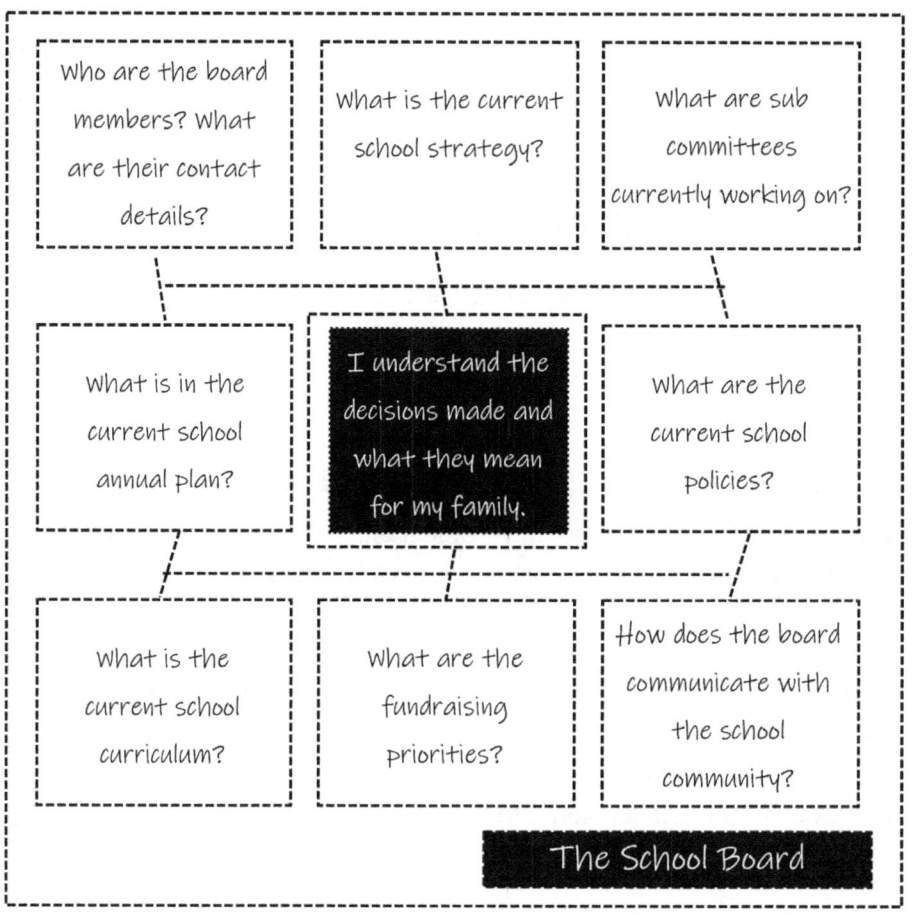

This is going to take a little time. You are doing important work together, to see the 'big picture' of your school.

Divide the nine questions, above, between you. Be clear about the goal in the centre box. The big picture should be easy to find and understand. And it should be of value to your children's education.

Agree on a time and date for your next meeting, to share what you've learned.

Here's a process you could use:

Information Gathering:
1. Collect necessary documents; they should be readily available
2. Highlight important points
3. Write any questions you have
4. If information isn't readily available, find out why
5. Prepare notes to share with the group.

Reminder: Every piece of information should be easily understood. Without understanding, being #1 for your children isn't possible.

Top-Down Spending Mandate

Spending and investing are two completely different concepts.

A New York City school district, with more than 40 schools, introduced a new reading initiative. The number of students in individual schools ranged from 250 to 1,200. Some schools embraced the new program; others chose not to participate. This didn't seem to matter. Every school received resources valued at about $30,000 for the program.

Shortly afterwards, I was assigned to District Head Office, to purchase resources for all schools from an additional $1,000,000 of funding for the new reading program. I suggested that, because a lot of schools already had more than enough reading resources, the funds could be reallocated. The money could be spent on other essential resources, including students' furniture and stationery in under-resourced schools. I was told the use of the funding was non-negotiable and the supplier of the first round of reading resources was the only one the district would purchase from.

Top-down processes that work in this way are costly and irresponsible. It's a 'one size fits all' approach. The district provided no room for individual schools to negotiate changes allowing them to acquire resources that would best support how they taught reading, or to find ways in which available funding could be used more effectively.

Distance between you and decision makers can be reduced if you are willing to speak out and they are willing to listen.

Wrap Up

- **LESSON 1:** There's a top-down bottom-up process to decision making.

LESSON 2:
Ownership and Collaboration

In **Lessons From The Sandpit**, you explored boundaries between home and school. That's what ownership and collaboration is all about too.

And it's natural you don't get everything right, all of the time. None of us does. What matters is that you take time to listen and remain open to different perspectives and to a range of solutions. This is especially the case when there's confusion over responsibilities about school education.

Some decisions made by the school can be problematic. Homework might eat into your family time or the cost of a school excursion might stretch your budget. A topic of study could be based solely on a teacher's opinion, while alternative views are ignored. You might make a decision, only to find it has been overridden by the school.

On the flip side, the more you expect from schools, the more you relinquish your responsibilities. That's when boundaries are blurred and relationships become strained.

Taking ownership of learning and teaching is everyone's responsibility. When that responsibility is recognised and accepted, cooperation and collaboration flow naturally. The less we dump on schools, the more they can focus on doing what they're genuinely supposed to do, and the more parents can raise their children well.

The school board can make sure very clear responsibilities and boundaries are in place for everyone in the community. It can also ensure bridges of support across the school and to other service providers.

With or without the school board, you hold the key.

PAIN POINTS

Are you familiar with the phrase *scope creep*? It's commonly used in project management to describe uncontrolled change and extra requirements that haven't been planned. It usually causes budget blow-outs. Scope creep applies to school education as well.

I describe it as the things parents request or expect of teachers that go beyond a teacher's responsibilities. Some examples of scope creep are: asking teachers to deal with conflict between parents and/or children; providing excessive after-hours support; or giving daily updates on academic achievement.

There's also what I call *scope overreach*. This is when teachers volunteer their time and services beyond their employment requirements. Some examples are: becoming involved in personal family matters; sharing personal information; counselling children; attending to matters meant for other professionals; and spending their own money on students.

There's also what I call *scope pressure*. It's when principals or government bodies make excessive top-down demands.

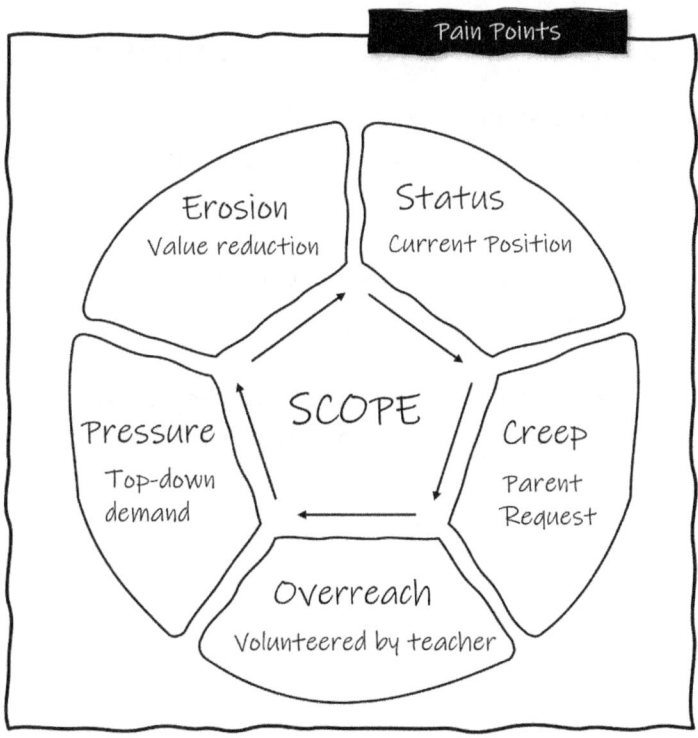

Any of these can reduce a teacher's productivity and lessen the value they provide. And, for you, there's less value in any time spent on the school board or committee, or helping with homework, if responsibilities, including responsibility for your children, are unclear.

Here are a few ways you can help:

- There's no easy way to say this: Don't do more than you should
- Don't expect more of your children's school than instruction in the agreed curriculum and support to source other essential services
- Be clear about your expectations and speak up whenever you identify overreach.

Taking your rightful place as leader in your children's education includes aligning school services with your expectations and vice versa. A collaborative approach to achieve what's best for your children is then possible.

You and everyone involved should be able to recognise and, respectfully, remove pain points.

WHEN HOME AND SCHOOL ARE UNDER ONE ROOF

Over the last twenty years, I've asked the following question of teachers and school leaders I've worked with: 'With hand on heart, would you confidently welcome the possibility of every teacher in your school teaching *your* children?'

Several decades and thousands of educators later, not one – I'll say it again, *not one* – teacher, anywhere in the world, has answered 'Yes'.

The message here is that you are not alone. Principals and teachers experience a blurring of boundaries – including a lack of ownership and collaboration – just as you do.

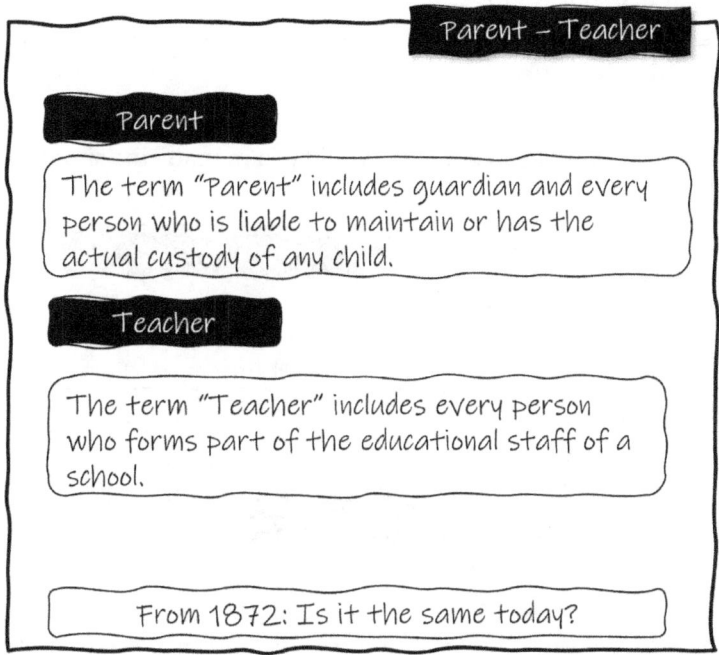

Clearly, teachers with children of school age can identify when their own children's education is compromised. For them, standing up, as parents first and colleagues second, isn't natural. That's why your advocacy will be so valuable to teachers who are also vulnerable parents. It can be challenging for them to establish healthy boundaries and assert their parental responsibility.

Any issues you raise also affects them, professionally and personally. You could call this a conflict of interest. I would much prefer to see you jump at these opportunities and support teachers to support you. The more you and other parents speak up, the stronger the pull toward a mutually respectful relationship between families and schools.

TAKING OWNERSHIP OF TRUST

How much do you trust others? When your children go on a playdate, is there agreement between you and the other parents about food, drink, entertainment, activities and conversation? What about when they join sporting clubs, faith groups and other social gatherings?

When rules are known and responsibilities are understood, life is so much easier. Don't you agree?

It can be awkward when boundaries are crossed. In most cases it's unintentional. You would assume adults wouldn't deliberately set out to undermine your authority, because it's something *you* wouldn't intentionally do.

If it did happen, though, what would you do? How would you manage the situation?

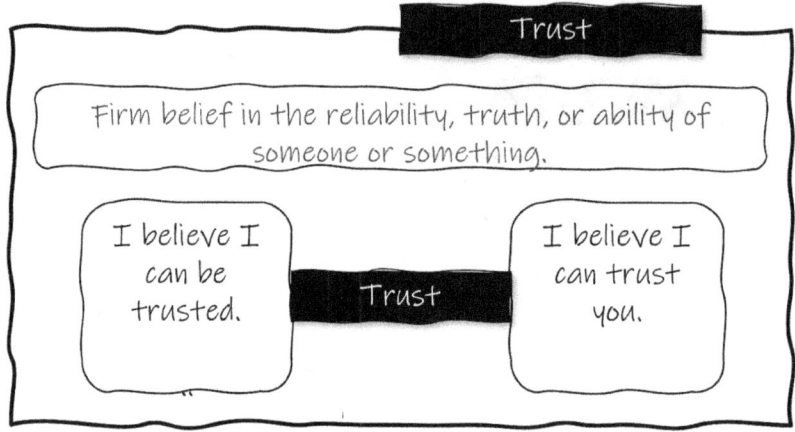

When I talk to parents about issues that are raised in schools, many say they manage them differently from the way they would in other settings.

That's a sign the 'childhood self' can pop up when we least expect it. It's amazing how often we become the child again when coming to terms with personal and shared responsibility in schools.

APLL Group

OWNING AND SHARING RESPONSIBILITY

By now you've gathered all the information about the school.

Now it's time to share and reflect on who's responsible for what.

1. Agree on the order in which information will be shared. You might need a few sessions to get through it all

2. Share information and questions

3. List any final questions and any confusing definitions or major points the group mentions.

Make sure everyone in your group understands the information you've gathered and what needs clarification.

You'll all set for the APLL session in the next lesson. Well done.

This Isn't Above Board

When mid-year student report cards came out, Sze Ting learned that she was an 'it'. Instead of 'she' and 'her', gender neutral pronouns, including 'they', had been used in her report card. Sze Ting was most upset. The teachers began their comments with, 'Ting is...' This first sentence was then followed by, '*They...*' or, 'I've suggested Ting does X so *they* can...'

I understand some people make a conscious decision to use gender-neutral pronouns for their own personal identification. But, aside from the grammatical inaccuracy, I don't agree with their broad use at all.

My expectation is that the school respects my view and, more importantly, that the school respects my daughter. Using the pronouns 'they' and 'their' instead of 'she' and 'her' without my daughter's consent crossed boundaries and is totally inappropriate – especially when the school's motto is 'Educating Individuals'.

Although my primary responsibility was to my daughter, I was also a member of the school board. Here's how I decided to approach the situation:

1. Discuss the situation with my daughter
2. Reach agreement about our expectations
3. Research school policies and the department website
4. Request the principal address the conflict between my daughter's rights and the school's actions
5. Request the issue be raised at the next school board meeting, to agree on a strategy that respects the rights of all students and parents.

Here's what happened:

1. Sze Ting was keen for me to support her position
2. I could not find any policies or government announcements stating that gender-neutral report cards were to be used
3. I requested copies of the legislation, ministerial order and policy that stated gender neutral report cards were to be used
4. I requested confirmation of the school board's approval of the use of gender-neutral report cards; to my knowledge it hadn't been discussed
5. The principal confirmed there was no such legislation
6. At the next school board meeting, the issue was raised and it was put to me that the school board did not address issues regarding individual students. I held my ground and responded frankly and honestly by stating that my daughter must have been singled out regarding report cards. I asked for an answer as to why.
7. Fast forward a few weeks: an apology and a questionnaire were sent to parents. There was only one question; essentially asking whether parents were concerned about gender neutral report cards. The options were: 'yes', 'no', 'don't care'.
8. At the next board meeting, members were told the school had acted on the wishes of some students and parents.
9. Sze Ting's report card was corrected.

Was it emotional? Yes. But I still had to act rationally.

Wrap Up

- **LESSON 2:** Knowing what you are responsible for leads to collaboration

LESSON 3:
Strategy and Change

The report card incident is a classic example of the way schools can assume that parents will passively accept their actions. Most, if not all, school communities, still include parents who trust and accept, without question, that schools make all educational decisions. They still suffer from blind faith, fear or both.

There's also a relinquishment of values, critical thinking and responsibility on the part of parents. Busy lives, distractions, scope creep or wrong assumptions about responsibility can stop a parent from speaking up.

Then there's the matter of top-down pressure from the school board.

In these cases, pushback isn't expected. If, as a parent, you are frank and seek clarity, it can feel like you're on your own. But remember that pushback isn't about being confrontational. It's a matter of principle. Decisions that have an impact on *your* children are *your* business; that is beyond question.

Sometimes conflict over expectations will be resolved easily; at other times that will not be the case.

The bottom line is that a school's strategy can alleviate these pain points. And, when plans and tactics support the school's strategy, frankness can have even more value.

THE SCHOOL STRATEGY

The best school board is one that is like you: honest, frank and clear about its responsibility for the education services your family will receive. The direction or strategy agreed by the school is set with the understanding that school staff are employees and you are the parents. You do not work *for* schools – schools work *with* you.

The board then sets out a plan – usually every year – that details how the school will work towards achieving its strategy. The plan includes responsibilities of individuals and teams, or sub-committees established to achieve specific tasks within a preferred time frame. It's then up to these teams and individuals to take action.

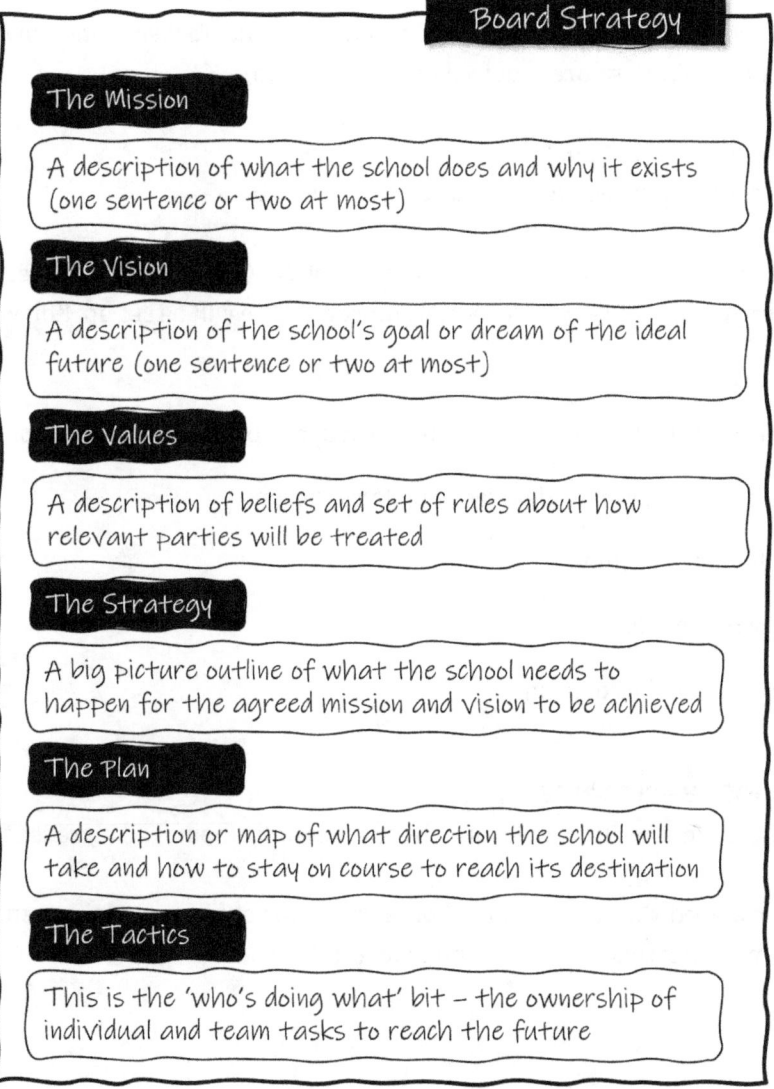

STRATEGY AND THE SCHOOL COMMUNITY

Everyone in the school community has a responsibility to contribute to the strategy. Day-to-day actions and decisions, including those of the principal, must reflect this agreed strategy. When the strategy is communicated well and understood, and all play their parts, it's a win for everyone. If the strategy is hidden in a cupboard, lacks detail or isn't understood, it's a loss for most.

Strategy Samplers

Let's look at two different schools. Can you understand each school's vision and how each school plans to achieve it? What contributions are required and from whom?

ELEMENTARY SCHOOL A – 2022-2025
Strategy: Become a leading school in competitive sport by 2025.

Plan A for 2023: Resurface the basketball court at a cost of $10,000. Funds for the resurfacing will come from donations and fundraising event. A special sub-committee will be set up: Kon will be chairperson.

Tactics:
- Kon and Grant to call local businesses for cash donations and silent auction items.
- Ahmad to organise flyers and advertising for the event.
- Blake to MC on the evening.
- Bev to rally parent volunteers.
- Amber to arrange the catering.

ELEMENTARY SCHOOL B – 2022-2025
Strategy: By 2025, students' writing, measured by teacher judgement, will increase from 88% to 94%.

2023 Plan: Further embed the school's model of learning for students to take responsibility for their learning and communicate this to parents and teachers.

ELEMENTARY SCHOOL A

The school board has clearly documented the school's vision. Everyone in the community knows that in four years the school will be recognised as a leader in competitive sport. There are plans for 2023. Plan A is for the improvement of facilities – in this case, the basketball court. Everyone knows the sub-committee is responsible and sub-committee members knows precisely what their contribution is.

It's fair to say principles of ownership and collaboration are valued at the school. If there are changes in staffing or committee membership, others can slide easily into the role, to complete unfinished tasks.

ELEMENTARY SCHOOL B

The school board strategy is to improve student's writing by 6% over 4 years. The students tell parents and teachers how they will improve. The school community will know if student writing has improved by opinions provided by the teachers.

The school's approach to education is based on students taking responsibility for their learning. There is no expectation of teachers to teach. In the four years of this strategy, at least 50% of the students expected to improve will be in secondary school by 2025. The focus on improvement in English is important. The strategy has little value.

TOP DOWN AND BOTTOM-UP CHANGE

Confusion over how much innovation can come from a school board and how much control a government has over schools seems unclear. Adding to the confusion is the impact of change.

Would you believe that, over the 13 years your children are involved in school education, there could be as many as 30 elections held? Let's see: 13 school council elections; 5 for the local council; 7 at state level; and potentially 5 federal elections. Yes, that's 30 elections!

These cause a sense of urgency with political timetables and campaign promises. Industries become involved. Grant money is splashed around. Promises are made. Some are kept and others broken.

Enthusiasm for change can cloud the need for school-wide consistency.

On the other hand, a rigid 4-year vision can mean new items are added to an already crowded plan. Either way, it seems there's little chance of successfully achieving any strategy.

Then there's change that happens in your home and throughout the school. Students and families leave, staff go on leave, are promoted or retire. New staff come in. Budgets change and there is unplanned progress or unforeseen upheaval.

Perhaps a balance between national consistency and local innovation is possible. Keep that one up your sleeve.

MANAGING CONFLICTING BELIEFS IN THE STRATEGY

Imagine school communities with hundreds of teachers, a thousand or more children and several thousand parents? You won't always agree with board decisions.

How you manage difference need not mean you have to be directly involved at board level. It does mean, however, you should understand the lines of communication between the board and your children. Your aim is for your children to have the best possible outcomes at school. How you support that might not always look the same, but it must be understood by your children's direct line of communication – their teacher.

School relationships can change and with change there will always be challenges.

CONFLICT SAMPLER

You believe that students should be promoted after achieving an agreed standard. The system (government) says it's ok for students to progress, despite their capabilities. Your school is divided but goes with the system's approach.

Here's some of the impact of that action:

- Teacher workload is overwhelming, and the range of student capability widens; it simply isn't manageable
- There are fewer whole class teaching experiences and one-on-one teaching time, when needed, is extremely rare. You become frustrated and send your child to a tutor
- The principal doesn't keep the school board informed. There's a belief that what happens in classrooms is not part of the strategy

- The school board goes about approving payments and rewriting policies. There's no understanding of the financial waste, the pressure on teachers, or the consequences for your child.

What should you do?

1. Nothing

2. Let the system push you around. After all - there's nothing you can do about it - it's just how it is

3. Keep paying for tutors and hope for the best.

You don't need to have all the answers. And you don't need to feel that a school strategy, no matter how good or bad is set in stone. None of these options, though, seem fair to anyone. Fortunately, there's another option. Your APLL group. This is the very reason why I encourage your participation.

APLL Group

WHAT ARE THE OPTIONS?

You've done your research on polices, strategy and the board.

The findings have been shared.

You've made a list of questions and you know what needs to be clarified.

The next step is to communicate with the board.

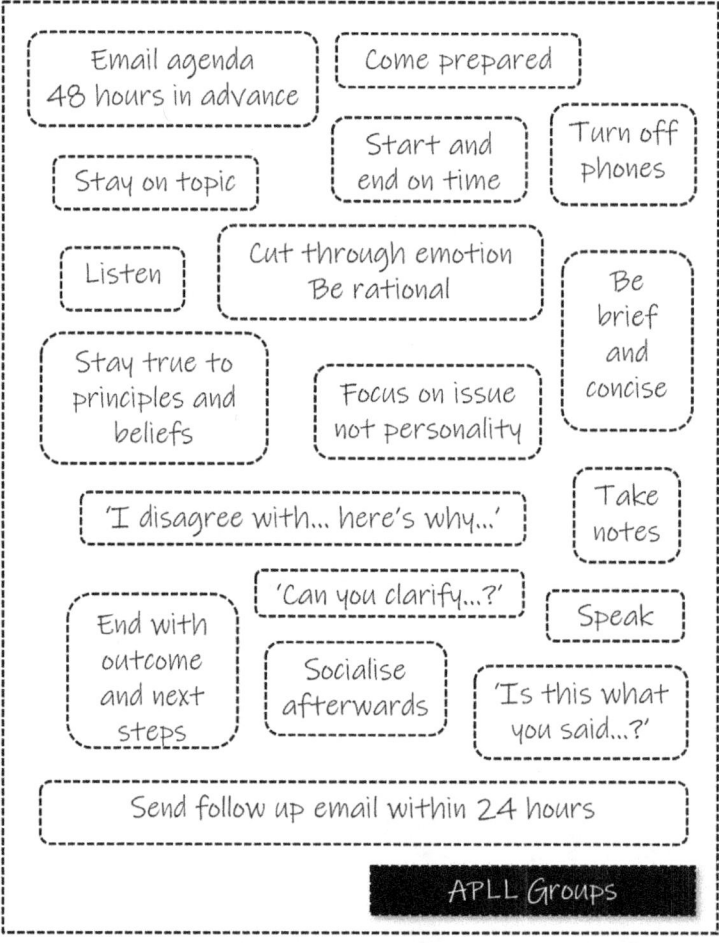

If you bombard the board with everything, there could be pushback.

If you do nothing, everybody loses.

Here's my suggestion: go right back to Lesson #1.

In it, you were introduced to a shared language of agreement. You've since read about and explored what makes this such an essential first principle.

It makes sense then that your group's first step in taking any recommendations or requests to your school board begins with your experience of a shared language of agreement.

Providing evidence of your group's confusion or disagreement over what is meant by certain words or concepts in the school documents you have explored and your approach to resolution sets a very high bar that would be difficult for anyone on the school board to ignore.

It's a proactive, honest and rational representation of how your APLL group and other school parents might see things.

Your group's desired outcome is an adjustment to any communication between families and the school that compromises the success of the school's strategy. Undoubtedly, your school board shares the same goal.

As for the plan and the tactics, you'll need to guarantee an agenda item at a school board meeting; that's up to your group. No two APLL groups are the same.

Just remember, if a document, direction or recommendation can't be understood, it can't be agreed to or fulfilled. The more significant support there is for a shared language of agreement, the better chance all families have of getting the most out of your school's mission and vision.

This visual and your experience in exploring school documents could be a further introduction to your APLL group.

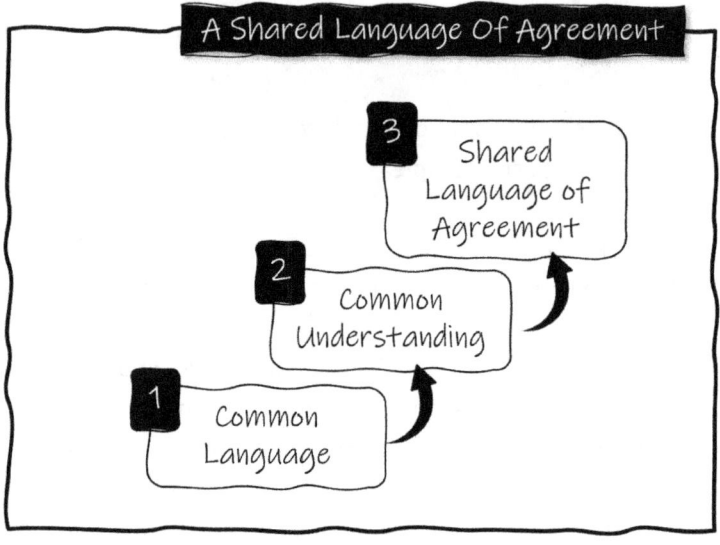

Finance and the School Board

At a school board meeting I advised the board that finance wasn't my strength, and that I would be grateful to receive clarification on some matters related to the finance report.

The principal stated that he had an accounting background and that school finance reports weren't always easy to follow, even for him.

I wasn't willing to approve the finance reports without understanding the following items:

- $7,000 spent on catering
- $32,000 in 'other' expenses (no details provided)
- $4,000 payment toward a printer that did not appear with leases or assets
- The funding agreement for the construction of a new school building on nearby parkland.

In addition, all computers – including the office computers – were marked as 'unseen' (missing) in the audit report.

The office manager responsible for preparing the documents said she didn't have the details, even though the finance committee had met immediately before the school board meeting and approved the items.

I had never fully understood financial records but clearly I knew that school funding is intended to improve student outcomes. I realised I should have spoken up much sooner, at previous meetings. This was an enormous mistake to have made.

Wrap Up

- **LESSON 3:** Everyone contributes to a school's mission and vision.

LESSON 4:
Education Services

Decisions about the school curriculum are part of the top-down, bottom-up process. Even so, they're only sometimes part of the school strategy. That's because government and leaders make some decisions and others are made at the school level. And, as you've learned, election cycles can wreak havoc on what schools do and don't do.

Are you clear about the curriculum that you want your children to be taught at school? What about outside school hours?

What the government demands and provides is often very different from your school community's needs and wants. Only some people agree, so the role of the school board becomes somewhat murky. Generally, it has become so vague that school boards no longer understand the strength of their position or have relinquished their responsibility.

As you know, a school board is responsible for setting the 'big picture' goals for the school – its strategy. The agreed path to achieving those goals and the *who will do what* – that is, the tactics – support this strategy.

At least, that's how it should be.

It makes sense, then, that your school strategy should align directly with the curriculum on offer. This brings us right back to needs and wants. Who decides?

WATCH THE GATEKEEPER

Gatekeeping happens when an individual or a group controls access to information about something. In the case of schools, it is usually finances or correspondence, but there can be other things. The reason for withholding the information is anyone's guess.

Regardless, the curriculum and your family are smack bang in the middle.

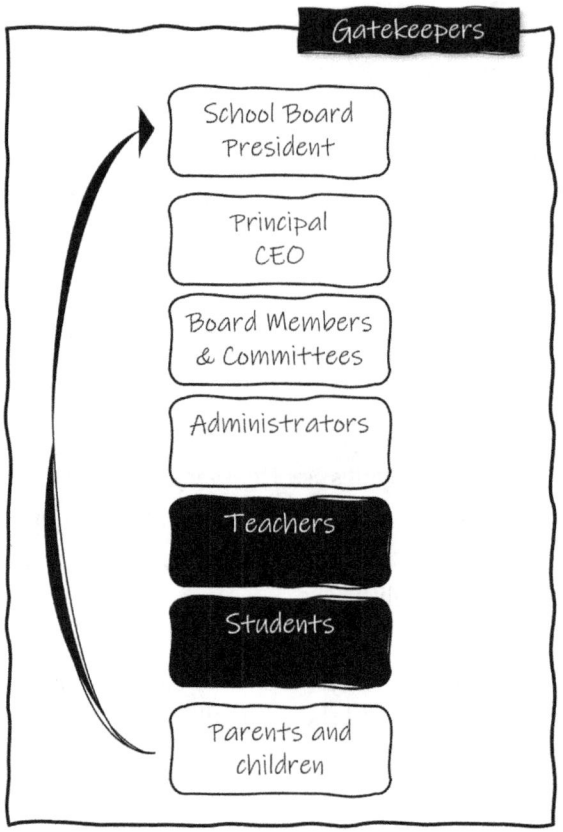

Chances are any of the people in this visual could be gatekeepers. Now, with all you know about school education, I'm sure alarm bells are going off.

Look at this strategy statement from a school's 4-year strategic plan.
By the end of the strategic plan, 95% of children will have achieved, in a calendar year, the equivalent of one level of growth in English and Mathematics, as measured by teacher judgement and evidenced growth in life skills.

This goal cannot be measured so it can never be achieved. Unfortunately, this is extremely common in schools. It feeds gatekeepers.

On the flip side, statements like these can have great value for you. They provide an indication of where change is needed and where conversations can begin.

A GAP IN LOGIC

Some believe children should be entitled to everything the most expensive school in the country offers. Some are of the opinion that more resources should be poured into schools where children are perceived to be disadvantaged – because English is their second language, or because of disability, distance from a city centre, or race. Others think greater investment in schools that teach the *best and brightest* students is a priority.

Not everything can be measured in numbers (quantitative) and not everything can be measured in by perceived value (qualitative). Even so, we have become complacent about curriculum in general.

The way things are at present, there is huge gap between what the national curriculum says and what is actually taught. That gap needs to be closed. On the other hand, if we close the gap entirely, there is no flexibility. We'd have total top-down government control. That's too frightening to contemplate. If we were to close the gap while keeping some options open, that would be a better way forward.

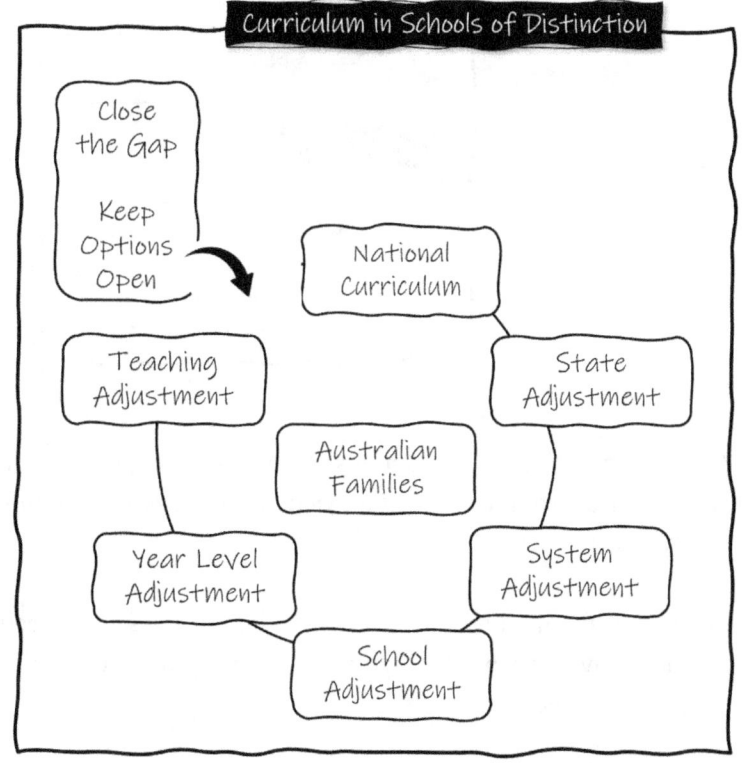

CLOSE THE ADJUSTMENT GAP AND KEEP OPTIONS OPEN

You know about the four areas of capability and that every community has people of varying capability in each area. Here they are again:

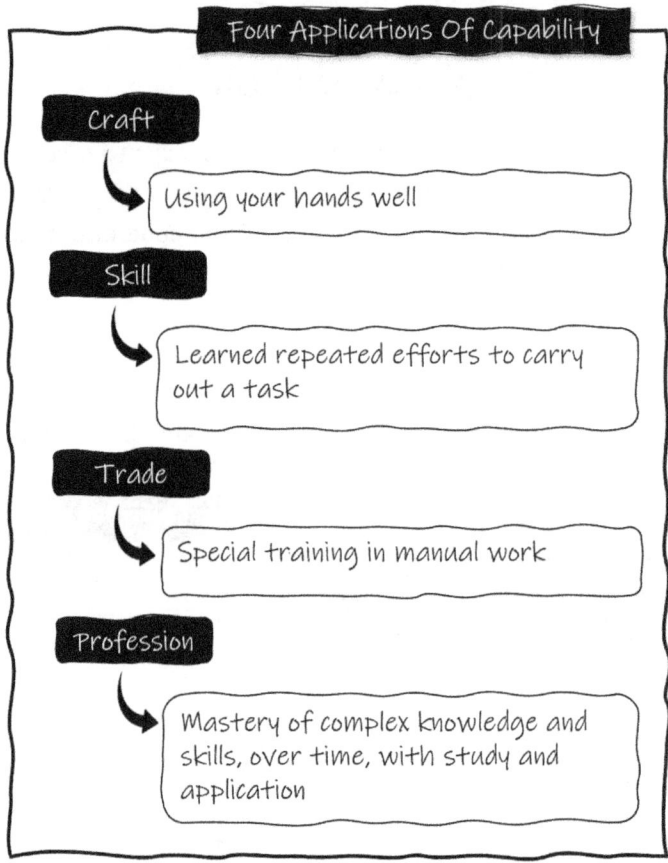

You also know that fundamental skills and knowledge apply to all of them. The teaching and assessment of these from a specified curriculum ensures equal opportunity looks the same in every school. That's logical.

Having a swimming pool, rowing club, kitchen classroom, orchestra, sound studio and bottomless pit of funds in every school, isn't logical. Personal goals can be different, and so can types of resources and teacher capabilities.

LESSON 4: EDUCATION SERVICES

How about this for a strategy?

The establishment of an Education Investment Fund (IEF) that places families at the centre of all decision making. In every school, three areas of curriculum could be offered, one of which would be compulsory and the other two taken flexibly, over time. Families apply allocated funds to the flexible curriculum areas on the condition that the agreed and measurable specified curriculum is achieved.

What does it look like?

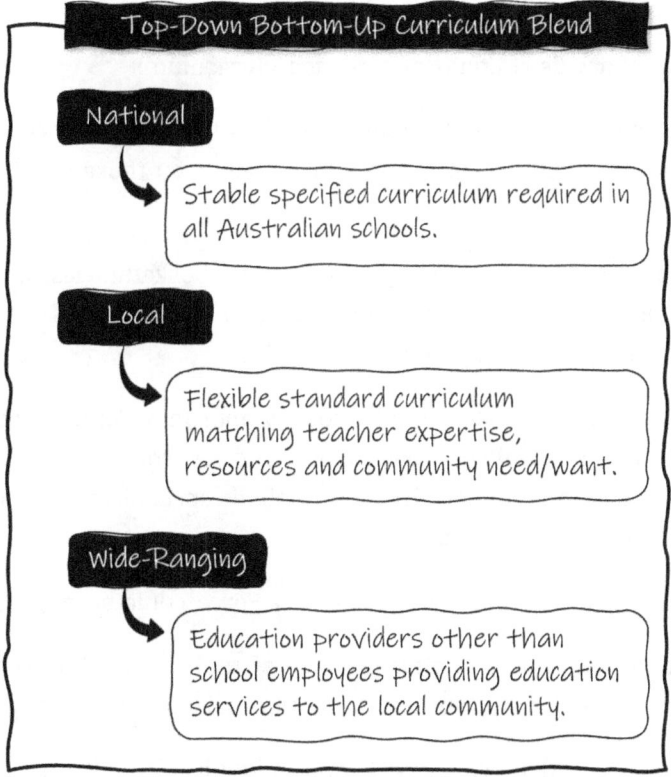

National Curriculum

All *Australian schools* are required to provide a specified curriculum in English, Mathematics, Fitness and Physical Education and Western Civilization. This is a measurable and stable curriculum with schools inspected quarterly, to monitor capabilities and provide support.

Local Curriculum

Every *Australian school* chooses the optional standard curriculum to match school resources and community need – for example, Art, Drama, IT and various sciences. The content is decided by the school board.

Wide-Ranging Curriculum

Every family can flexibly access education from other service providers, including those who hire the school premises.

Here are some examples of a wide-ranging, or extended, curriculum:

- Out of school hours 'Mother and Daughter' and 'Father and Son' classes, once available to provide health and sexuality education and delivered by those qualified to do so, could be reintroduced

- One of Ting's schools leased half their gymnasium for basketball lessons offered by local clubs and the other half to gymnastics clubs. What facilities in your school are currently being leased and how could this option be expanded?

- Adult English classes were once available to new migrants. Families would attend the school after hours and parents would gain the support and assistance of their children during family English lessons. Does your community have qualified specialists who could meet the needs or interests of families after school hours?

- Cadet Units, funded and delivered by the Defence Force, could be established

- Family education classes might offer a range of topics, including respectful relationships, financial management, healthy eating, meditation, grief and loss, or travel

- After-school tutoring and instrumental lessons might be also offered.

TEACHERS AND THE CURRICULUM

I sometimes wonder whether the school education system is just a bad dream and one day we'll wake up and it will be as it could and should be.

Remember when we compared two schools that offered different PE and other services? That's pretty much what schools are like today.

School board members can't tell you what is, or could be, on offer if they don't even know.

You'll also recall reading about how music was a one year elective for me at teacher's college, yet I was still responsible for teaching music to my students.

Despite their capabilities, or lack thereof, many 'generalist teachers' still cover all curriculum areas, including music.

Suppose teachers need more academic and practical experience in music yet are allocated a teaching role; the study, interest, competence and future options in music for every student in that school are compromised. Furthermore, time is not used wisely, taxpayers are paying for poor standards, and parents are juggling time and funds for after-hours music tutors.

A better option would be for the school board to self-employ a specialist for music, choir, band, orchestra and the coordination of community-enriching experiences.

With grants provided by the Federal government or fundraising and donations through community and business groups, music need not be an out-of-field, poorly delivered extra but a highly regarded opportunity for students.

With national, local and wide-reaching curriculum options, the school board would have a more explicit purpose for improving school performance and facilities. Your school board could take educators off the 'They can teach everything thrown at them' pedestal and place them on the firm ground of 'This is the expertise our school offers'.

You know what that would mean. You would have a School of Distinction™!

APLL Group

BOARD SUPPORT

There are several ways you can contribute to the school board.

Consider these options and share your thinking:

1. **Further learning.** Learn about any available board training endorsed by the current board. Explore other options

2. **Join the board.** Nominate as a parent representative. No special skills are required. Representing the school community means sharing views, needs or concerns, on their behalf, and making the best possible decisions for them

3. **Join a sub-committee.** Your school board will have several subcommittees, each focusing on specific areas within the school. A few possibilities are: fund raising; events; finance; and facilities. It's also a good way to be more hands on.

4. **Set up a meeting roster.** Your APLL group meetings are powerful vehicles for parent support. You can work collectively to put proposals together and get to know a broader range of school parents. You can set up a roster so that two parents attend each school board meeting, as visitors. School boards should encourage visitors and make them welcome. Parents who attend can take notes and report back to your group. They will also have an opportunity to raise matters in general business. A roster is a great way to take the pressure off busy parents without them having to relinquish the opportunity for a 'bird's eye view' of board decision making.

5. **Network with other APLL groups.** Get to know other Australian Parents Leading Learning and find out more about how they are contributing to their schools. Some of the issues they are addressing might be similar to yours. Knowing about potential difficulties in advance often means you can prevent them. Sharing your successes, too, can mean success for other schools.

6. **Tips for busy parents.**
   Understand the school strategy and the services provided.
   Be aware of the contribution you are required to make.
   Seek clarification, when necessary.
   Contribute, wherever possible.

1. Further learning
2. Join the board
3. Join a sub-committee
4. Set up a meeting roster
5. Network with APLL groups
6. Tips for busy parents

Board Support

Do the Research

At one of my daughter's schools, the principal was completing a PhD, on top of her full-time workload. She shared this openly and it's fair to say the school community was thrilled to have a leader so dedicated to education.

Fast forward a few months, though, and things had changed. As part of her studies and with the help of the university and teachers in the school, the principal had woven a new approach into the school curriculum. A research program also began and it involved every student in the school. Parents, however, were *not* notified.

To make matters worse, the school board had secretly approved this. It caused a huge division within the ranks of school leadership and the parent body. And rightly so. The school board had placed the principal's career, and the kudos it would bring them, ahead of the children and parents.

A small group of parents pursued the matter. News rapidly spread of our stand for families.

The principal and the university then did a backflip and sent families a letter, outlining details of the research project. An opt in or opt out option was included.

Had the principal and school board been honest from the outset, the research and new curriculum might well have provided benefits to the school. Instead, the main outcome was a loss of trust.

Wrap Up

- **LESSON** 4: There's room for flexibility alongside a specified curriculum.

LEARNINGS FROM PART 3:
Lessons From The Boardroom

LESSON 1: There's a top-down bottom-up process to decision making.

LESSON 2: Knowing what you are responsible for leads to collaboration.

LESSON 3: Everyone contributes to a school's vision and mission.

LESSON 4: There's room for flexibility alongside a specified curriculum.

Taking the Lead

Nike. ***Just Do It!*** This tagline is part of the branding for the world's number one sneakers. Branding showcases what's different about a particular product or service and helps build a loyal market. It establishes a product's 'point of difference'.

Everyone knows Nike is a fitness wear company. It doesn't need to market the benefits of its sneakers compared with stilettos. Nike needs to distinguish itself from other manufacturers of sports footwear.

Nike came up with this point of difference: *We listen to our customers.* The company 'proves' this by making unique Nike products for the world's greatest sporting heroes.

You are a customer of the education system. You are the world's greatest hero and influencer in your children's education.

Imagine what school communities will be like when every school says, *'We listen to our customers.'*

You're about to make it happen. With your influence and support your school board will say 'No' to mediocre school education and 'Yes' to being a *School of Distinction*™.

Taking the Lead

YOU ARE A CENTRE OF INFLUENCE

Wow! Think about everything you have read, questioned, jotted down and shared with your APLL group. You are now a leading centre of influence. Isn't that great?

You know about fair and equal school education. And you've done your homework. Let's put it all together, now, in one neat package.

Here's how we'll go about it. We will:

1. Do a quick reflection
2. Revisit the principles from each chapter
3. Apply the principles to a logical framework
4. Choose how to share the framework with your school board.

A QUICK REFLECTION

You and your children are at the centre of every top-down and bottom-up decision, even when you haven't participated in that decision.

For example, a decision is made at one school. The decision gains momentum. Other schools start taking things on, then more schools and so on. Before you know it, these things are happening in *your* school.

A poorly made decision that does not have parent support, however, can have dire consequences. When this happens, you have lost your voice. The opportunity for collaboration has been erased.

Consider this situation for a moment:
A computer for every student

Think back to your reading about computers and smartphones. They have become the acceptable norm in schools. This is a good example of a decision that had various repercussions.

Government had a 'big picture' idea and then handed the cost, the risk of mental health problems and screen addiction and most other consequences over to you. We're now doing everything possible to overcome the difficulties this situation has caused: more programs in schools, more interventions through anti-bullying campaigns and more counselling services. Sometimes, one idea becomes a major problem in need of a fix.

Now consider a scenario where parents take the lead in the process of decision making:
Optional out of school hours activities

Perhaps, for our purposes, some parents from your community want to set up a Cadet Unit. You attend a board meeting, as a parent representative, and propose an idea for an opt-in out of school hours activity for families in your community. You present details of a Commonwealth School Cadet Unit, established through the Department of Defence. The Commonwealth Government will rent your school property for the after-school sessions, where the children will learn discipline, resilience, teamwork, goal setting and leadership – in real time and for real purposes.

Your idea attracts the attention of other parents and decision-makers and gradually other schools take up the idea. Improvement in the lives of children and families begins to unfold because you shared an idea with your school board.

Perhaps in a slightly different way, that is exactly what you're doing right now! You are making a difference.

THE PRINCIPLES WE HAVE EXPLORED

Learnings From Lessons

The Sandpit

Lesson 1: A shared language of agreement is critical for having clarity, talking things through and getting things done.

Lesson 2: The purpose of schools is to *help you* prepare your children to live a happy and responsible life.

Lesson 3: Schools must provide the same basic service to every family, regardless of its composition.

Lesson 4: The rule of law is represented in schools through rules and policies that must be agreed to and understood by everyone in the community.

Lesson 5: Families might see privacy and responsibility differently but agreement on these concepts is essential in schools.

Learnings From Lessons

The Classroom

Lesson 1: A school's philosophy should be easy to understand. It should respect your right to fulfil your responsibility for your children's education and your children's right to have your protection.

Lesson 2: Schools and teachers can value different approaches to teaching and learning.

Lesson 3: A university teaching degree isn't a licence to teach anything to anyone.

Lesson 4: There are different types of curriculum.

Lesson 5: Being literate means being able to produce, understand and use English to interact in the right way with anyone.

Lesson 6: A non-negotiable specified curriculum can sit alongside negotiable electives and other education services.

Lesson 7: Knowing what to measure, and how, is an essential principle of teaching and learning.

Lesson 8: Funding a non-negotiable specified curriculum and honouring diverse abilities can remove school inequality.

Lesson 9: Electronic devices are not essential for learning.

Lesson 10: Families make adjustments to home-school-work and family life to fit around inflexible school hours.

Learnings From Lessons

The Boardroom

Lesson 1: There's room for flexibility alongside a specified curriculum

Lesson 2: Everyone contributes to a school vision and mission.

Lesson 3: Knowing what you are responsible for leads to better collaboration.

Lesson 4: There's a top-down bottom-up process to decision making.

APPLYING THE PRINCIPLES TO A FRAMEWORK

The school should have in place a framework that can be seen clearly and communicated effectively to all members of the community. The essential elements or components in the framework are the *First Principles* that underlie the relationship between families, the school and the wider community.

And when these principles are understood by all, and put into practice, that's when it's possible to have a 'School of Distinction™'.

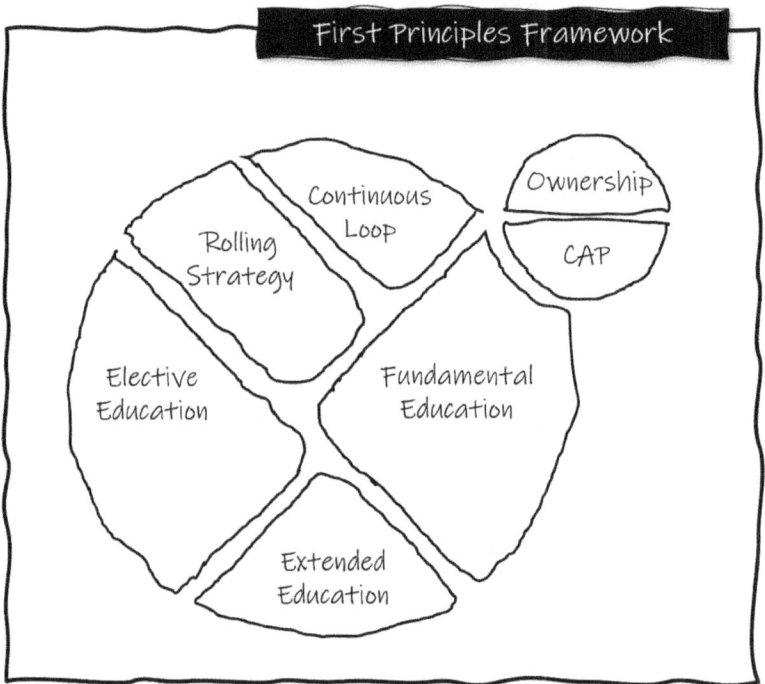

Ownership Brief
Everyone in the school community understands and agrees on their roles and responsibilities.

Collaborative Action Plan (CAP)
A community of trust enables collaboration between family, school and community.

Rolling Strategy
The school board, in consultation with the school community, develops a vision and a plan that are understood and agreed.

Continuous Loop
Adjustments are made to the strategy, plans and tactics when change occurs.

Fundamental Education
An agreed explicit and measurable non-negotiable curriculum in English, Maths, Fitness and Physical Education and Western Civilization is equally available to all students.

Elective Education
Students have optional opportunities to apply fundamental skills and knowledge, with school resources available.

Extended Education
Students and families have options to participate in education services offered outside the specified and elective curriculum.

SHARING THE FRAMEWORK

You now have enough tools in your toolbox to share your ideas about your School of Distinction™.

First, you have this book and everything you've learned about school education, including **Lessons From The Sandpit, Lessons From The Classroom** and **Lessons From The Boardroom**.

You also have your APLL group and all the charts, principles and ideas that have flowed on from your conversations.

You know how to be frank, you know how to be honest and you have a new vantage point, as a parent who can 'take the lead' in your children's education.

Here are your next steps:

1. Share your vision with your family

2. Talk about the possibilities this flexible opportunity can bring

3. Host a APLL group chat. You can offer your ideas about what an ideal school might look like, hear from others and formulate a shared vision

4. Start an action plan for taking your vision further.

If you have any doubts, remember that what you are about to embark on is already happening in other places. Children are pursuing goals in elite sport and attending school. Some families choose home schooling and have support from education services, including schools. Families in remote areas are accessing distance education. Some children attend school while living with debilitating illness. And some schools enthusiastically share their premises with community groups.

Flexibility is already available and working well; it's just been hiding. You are no longer out of the picture.

Just as importantly, other parents have read this book and are creating schools of distinction for their children and their communities.

I know you will take part in an extraordinary movement for innovation and change. You have already begun.

Schools have value. Teachers are important. Children are students some of the time. You are a parent all of the time.

To educate – bring up young persons from childhood, to form their habits, manners, intellectual and physical attributes includes 'educare' – to train or mould and 'educere' – to lead out.

Every school and its community make up a unique unit. A well-functioning, supportive and inviting school board will welcome your input, respect your position and have established and agreed to boundaries and bridges between family and school 'education'.

Most importantly, by advocating for your position of responsibility as parents, you will never regret being the number one influencer in your children's education.

You're it! Numero uno!

A Final Word

Life evolves in patterns, cycles, routines and habits.
We inherit success, failure, error and wisdom.
We pass them on.

An extraordinary cycle in my family life unfolded while writing this book.

First, I learned that my father's great uncle William Nicholas Lacey, was a premiership player for Carlton FC and an articled clerk. Just one examination shy of becoming a barrister, he gave it all away to become a schoolteacher. Later, he became the Headmaster of Maryborough Grammar School and introduced Aussie rules football to country Victoria.

Then I found some of Dad's papers, tucked away in a suitcase. Among them were the minutes of some meetings held at the primary school my older brother John and I attended, and Dad's correspondence with the then Director of Education on various matters, including a request for assurance that our school would receive promised resources and services.

My father was a trailblazer, leading a team of dedicated parents, and meeting with politicians and bureaucrats as he represented school families.

To be educated: that was the vision of our forefathers and mothers. They built our schools and universities, our places of worship and our homes. They built our nation.

It's now my vision and yours. In years to come, it will be our children's. And through us, and our children, our ancestors will live on.

Your Legacy

We begin our life with two biological parents.

We end our life alone.

In the middle we change, through learning and teaching.

We move from the unknown to the known.

We become educated.

Go with confidence. Stay safe and God bless.

Keep in Touch

Let me know how you are going.

Talk to me. Write to me.

Follow my regular newsletters

https://cheryllacey.substack.com

Join me at online and live events.

Keep up to date with ideas for Australian Parents Leading Learning.

www.cheryllacey.com

Most of all, please keep in touch.

I'm always here to help.

cheryl@cheryllacey.com

www.linkedin.com/in/cheryl-lacey-dsj

As we embark on creating Schools of Distinction™, we need national consistency. I invite you to combine your advocacy for local innovation with my efforts and those of others. Help me to establish a *National Independent Board of Education* and reintroduce *Teachers' Colleges*. Talk to your APLL group about this quest and contact me when you're ready to learn more.

That's my vision, and I trust it's yours too.

cheryl@cheryllacey.com

First Principles On Education™

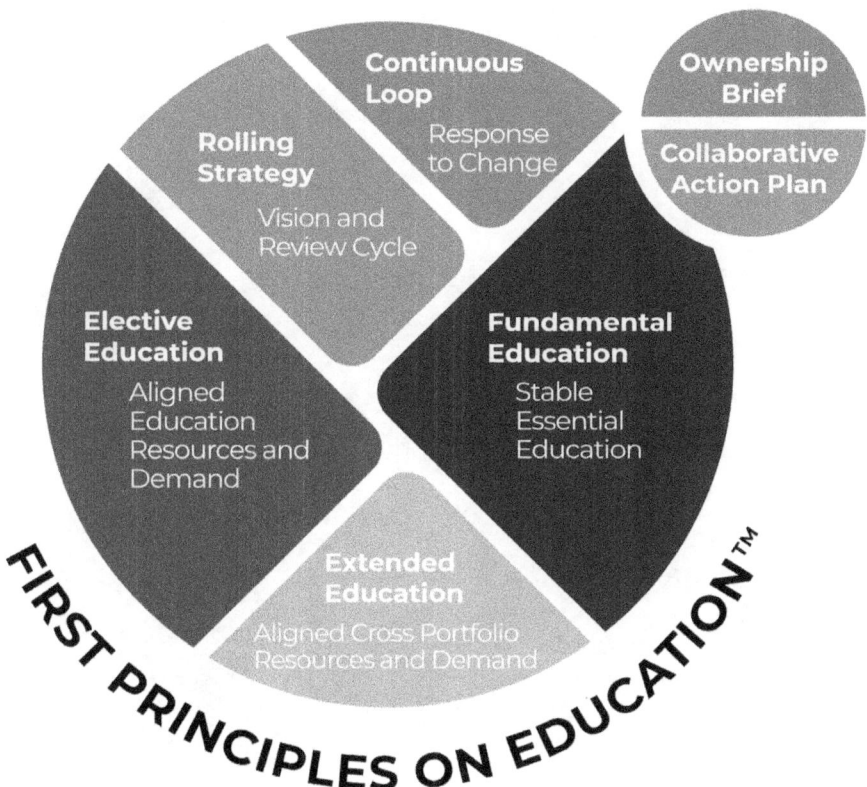

First Principles on Education™ are building blocks for stability, innovation and change.

The framework connects where you are now and the result you are looking for; it also shows you how to get there.

Applying the framework helps your school board maintain its focus on the impact of current services on the school community and how innovation and change can be introduced.

Schools that apply First Principles On Education™ and adopt its framework become Schools of Distinction™.

For more information on First Principles on Education™ visit **www.firstprinciplesoneducation.com**

You'll also find a link to this framework at **www.cheryllacey.com**

Glossary

40/12 principle – a system comprising 40 weeks of work and 12 weeks of vacation time

Achieved curriculum – the combined input and outcome of teaching and learning

Actual curriculum – what has been delivered by the teacher

Assessment – the collection, review and measurement of information about educational programs and services

Common law – a collection of past decisions made by the judiciary

Comprehend – to understand

Concept – an abstract idea

Constitution – a set of principles that acts as a legal basis for determining how laws and governance of an organisation, state or nation are to be formulated

Core curriculum – an essential course of study, compulsory for all

Craft – a skill involving working with your hands

Curriculum – a course of study, comprising core and optional components

Decode – to convert coded messages into meaningful language

Duty of care – the duty to behave responsibly and avoid any harm that could knowingly be caused by your behaviour

Education – the action of teaching and learning

Fairness – impartial and just treatment

Gender neutral – conveying no characteristics (e.g. of roles and behaviours) that are based on gender

Hidden (Implicit) curriculum – learning that is not intended

Informed consent – consent given with full knowledge of the consequences

Instruction – the action of teaching

Intended curriculum – a course of study, designed, tested and published for official use

Ministerial order – an order made by a government minister

Out-of-field teaching – teaching in an academic subject or a grade level for which the teacher is not specifically qualified

Pedagogy – the art and science of teaching: the way educators approach their teaching

Personal attributes – knowledge, skills and qualities of individuals

Personalised learning – customised learning

Philosophy – the study of knowledge and thought; guiding principles for behaviour

Phonics – the relationship between letters and sounds, used in learning to read and write

Pinky promise – the most serious and sacred promise in the history of the world

Principle – a value or belief that influences and guides behaviour

Profession – the mastery and application of complex knowledge and skills in a specific area, gained through study and practical experience, over time

Professional attributes – knowledge, skills and attributes of the teaching (or other) profession

Reading – decoding and understanding written materials

School – a place of learning

Schooling – instruction received at school

Scope – the range and extent of combined objectives and contributions relevant to complete a project

Self-directed learning – processes that are controlled by learners

Skill – the result of learned repeated efforts to carry out complex tasks

Specified curriculum – agreed non-negotiable explicit and measurable statements of intent

Statutory law – written law that has been debated and agreed on by government

Student agency – where students exercise the ability and will to influence their own lives

Teacher judgement – a teacher's personal opinion or evaluation of student performance

Trade – an occupation requiring special training, usually in manual work

Vantage point – a position with a good view; a particular perspective

Wellbeing – a state of good mental and physical health

About the Author

Cheryl is a mother of two and an educationist.

Since beginning teaching in 1989, she has moved around and beyond classrooms, in Australia and overseas working to understand school education systems and the relationship between families and schools.

What she has observed and experienced first-hand is an absence of the critical distinction between 'student' and 'child'. This belief has been the driving force behind her family life, work and studies.

Your Children: Take the Lead on Their Education is Cheryl's latest publication. In it, she places parents where she believes they should be: firmly at the centre of all decision making.

Cheryl has a record of active involvement in community service, most notably her longstanding membership of the Rotary Club of Melbourne and her recognition as a Dame of the Order of St. John of Jerusalem, Knights Hospitaller.

She has recently completed postgraduate studies in Parental Alienation, as part of the first group of professionals world-wide to complete such a course.

Cheryl continues to write, speak and advise on the relationship between families and schools and how fundamental change begins locally.

www.ingramcontent.com/pod-product-compliance
Lightning Source LLC
Chambersburg PA
CBHW080408300426
44113CB00015B/2442